ROCK CLIMBS IN THE PYRENEES

Mallo Pison with the Puro on its left. Photo: A Harmon

ROCK CLIMBS IN THE PYRENEES

BY

DEREK L. WALKER

A selection of rock routes on the Pic du Midi d' Ossau
and the Pre-Pyrenees of Huesca province including
Riglos and Ordesa

CICERONE PRESS
MILNTHORPE, CUMBRIA

ISBN 1 85284 039 0
© Derek L. Walker 1990

Acknowledgements

This book is dedicated to my wife Chris for holding the fort while I was away enjoying myself, to my daughter Lisa for her willing help with translation and to my son Ellis for his encouragement.

To Dave Walsh for never-to-be-forgotten times on the big routes of the Ossau and Vignemale and to Iain Jones, Duncan Reade, Dave Gale and Chris Nunn for the big pushes on Riglos, new route information and their warm companionship whilst checking the routes.

Many of the sections of the book would not have been possible without the help of my Spanish 'Amigos,' Julio Armesta, Fernando Guzman and Enrique Villasur. Their love of the mountains and light hearted attitude (even when *in extremis*) has been an inspiration. Good ethics, hard climbing and hedonism can combine easily in their company.

Many thanks go to all the previous writers and to barmen throughout Huesca for their patience when I was transcribing descriptions kept in their establishments whilst drinking their wine into the early hours.

Derek L. Walker

CONTENTS

LIST OF DIAGRAMS

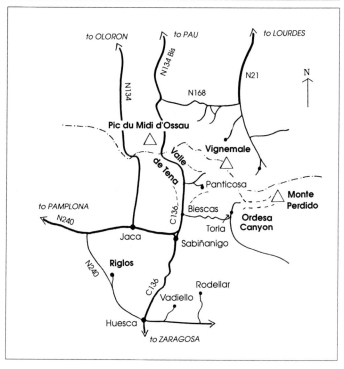

Map of the guidebook area

INTRODUCTION

'Sueño con los angeles.' Spanish expression.

This book is intended as an invitation to climbers to enjoy all that is best about rock climbing in the British style, sustained free moves with natural protection in the bigger arena of the Pyrenees and its environs. A 500m route on immaculate andesite leading to the summit slopes of a 3,000m peak is not uncommon on the Pic du Midi d'Ossau. A 300m route on hard sandstone in a 10-mile long, mile deep, mile wide canyon is representative of Ordesa while the towers and walls of Riglos growing out of the Spanish plain give 300m routes of stunning grandeur.

The Pyrenees have long been known as a Mecca for walkers and mountain scramblers, but they also offer excellent rock climbing in good weather, magnificent surroundings and with an almost total absence of crowds - at the time of writing. It is normal to have the route to oneself, common to have the face to oneself and occasionally the mountain also.

Three of the areas chosen for the book lie on a 25-mile arc which more or less follows the French-Spanish border and includes some of the highest and most spectacular of the Pyrenean summits: Midi d'Ossau, Palas, Balaitous, Grande Fache, Infierno, Vignemale, Taillon, Marboré, Perdido. Midway along the chord joining the ends of this arc is the tiny ski village of Panticosa, situated in the Spanish province of Huesca. This is an excellent central base for all the areas described: it has shops, bars, restaurants, tennis courts and a swimming pool. It is also a base in its own right for easy mountaineering and for smaller escuelas.

The Valle de Tena which contains Panticosa, the larger ski resort of Formigal and the campsites at Escarilla and Biescas may be reached from any of the channel ports in a day's drive via Bordeaux, Pau and the Col de Portalet. It is also possible to use public transport to Pau and then a succession of trains and buses over the Col du Somport to Canfranc, Jaca, Sabiñanigo and finally Panticosa.

The weather on the French side of the Pyrenean chain may be cloudy, particularly in the afternoons and the terrain one of lush steep-sided river valleys. The weather on the Spanish side is normally continuous sunshine and the terrain is more open, rolling and grassy. This combined with the low cost of food, drink and accommodation would seem to confirm the Spanish side as the ideal choice as base, both for climbers and camp followers.

The routes described offer a challenge to all climbers who perform at severe standard and upwards, who would like to attempt longer routes in a mountain setting but without the oppressive objective dangers found in areas of higher altitude. The increased length, ever present concern with route finding and time pressure to finish without benighting, add a further dimension to both the joy and thrill of the climbing experience. However, the descriptions chosen are for routes with little or no loose rock and only minor route finding difficulty.

Grades
The grading system adopted is the British numerical system for individual pitches, 4a, 5b, etc., and an adjectival system for the overall route. For longer routes however, British adjectives have not been used as the total problem presented by routes of 300m to 800m in length cannot be accurately equated to VS, E2, etc. The system in general use for alpine routes, shown below, has been adopted. (N.B. The English translation should not be equated with English grades.)

	Spanish	*French*	*English*
F	Facil	Facile	Easy
PD	Poco Dificil	Peu Difficile	A Little Difficult
AD	Algo Dificil	Assez Difficile	Rather Difficult
D	Dificil	Difficile	Difficult
MD or TD	Muy Dificil	Très Difficile	Very Difficult
ED	Extremadamente Dificil	Extremement Difficile	Extremely Difficult

+ and - is used to indicate shades of difficulty. Routes of D+ upwards should be considered as major undertakings because of length, difficulty, problems of escape etc.

Descriptions
A 'topo' system has been used for most routes and where the route is easy to follow a pitch by pitch written account has been omitted. The directions 'left' and 'right' have been used in the sense of direction of the climber either in ascent or descent. Compass points have been added in some cases. A 'star' system has been added to

indicate routes of high quality 'for that particular area.'

   *   A better than average route
   **   A very good route
   *** A route which stands comparison with the best of other areas

The book is divided into seven sections, one for each area, and each area into sub-sections to accommodate the faces described. The DESCENTS for all routes are described at the beginning of the section or sub-section containing the route.

Maps and Huts
A variety of maps are available for the area both in style and scale. The area is well served with bookshops (*librerias*) and maps will be found in many other shops also.

Maps which have proved useful are:-

Spanish   Federacion Espanola de Montanismo MM010
             Ordesa-Vignemale-Monte Perdido 1:25,000
             Mapa Topographico-Excursionista Piriheo Aragonés,
             Panticosa Formigal 1:25,000, Valle de Ordesa 1:40,000.
             The latter two contain other useful information
             about the area and its walks.

French   IGN Carte Touristique 273, 274, 275. 1:25,000.

The good weather and easy access to the crags makes huts unnecessary. It is left to those requiring a roof over their heads instead of a bivouac to consult their chosen maps.

Accidents and Emergencies
If external help is required in an emergency it is best to refer in the first instance to the nearest manned refugio. If a telephone is used then, in Spain contact the nearest Gardia Civil station, in France ring Oloron Ste Marie 59 39 00 49 or Argelès Gazost 62 97 07 70.

Spanish Glossary

Abierto	Open	Canal	Couloir
Aguja	Gendarme	Cantera	Quarry
		Cerrado	Closed
Barranco	Ravine	Chimenea	Chimney
Blanco	White	Circo	Amphitheatre
Brecha	Col	Clavija	Piton
Bruja	Witch	Collado	Col
		Cornisa	Ledge

Diedro	'Diedre'	Negra	Black
		Norde	North
Embalse	Reservoir		
Entosta	Large Flake	Oeste	West
Ermita	Hermitage, chapel		
Escuela	School	Panza	Bulge
Espelon	Buttress	Pared	Wall
Este	East	Playa	Town Square
		Pueblo	Village
Fisura	Crack		
		Repisa	Ledge
Hierba	Grass	Reunion	Belay
Ibon	Lake	Suerte	Luck
		Sur	South
Liberia	Bookshop		
Libro	Book	Techo	Overhang

TOPO SYMBOLS

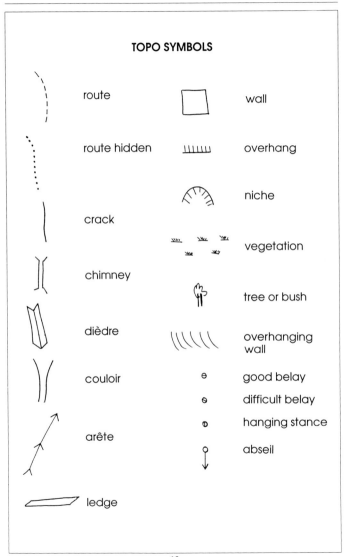

route		wall
route hidden		overhang
		niche
crack		vegetation
chimney		tree or bush
dièdre		overhanging wall
couloir		good belay
		difficult belay
		hanging stance
arête		abseil
ledge		

Grande Pic North Face, the upper half as seen from the walk in.
Photo: J. Armesta

PIC DU MIDI D'OSSAU   2,884m

The Pic du Midi d'Ossau is unquestionably a rock climber's mountain paradise. Its southern side gives high quality rock climbs in their own right, while its northern side has mountaineering routes involving good rock climbing, sufficiently far from civilisation to give a mountain feeling, yet close enough to roads to give ease of access. The peak is made of andesite, natural protection abounds and the altitude ensures ideal climbing temperatures during the summer months. Hard routes on the Pombie Wall may frequently be done comfortably in winter while the easier lines on the mountain give excellent winter outings.

The principal features of the Ossau massif are the Grand Pic and Petit Pic, separated by a large col, the Fourche. The Petit Pic, the more westerly of the two, is easily recognised by its sharp conical appearance, whilst the Grand Pic has a large sloping facet, the Rein de Pombie, leading to the summit from its East Ridge. The southern aspect of the Grande Pic has a very prominent gendarme, the Pointe de Aragon, and a smaller, lower but very important one, the Pointe Jean Santé. Lower still is the Aiguillette Jolly.

From the climber's point of view, the massif may conveniently be divided into a number of faces. The South-East Face of the Grand Pic, best approached from the Anéou pastures via the Lac de Pombie contains the Pombie Wall, a 500m sheer wall, as its main feature. This wall is bounded on its right (E) by the Couloir Pombie-Souzon and on its left (W) by the Couloir Pombie-Peyreget which runs beneath the Pointe de Aragon up to the Pointe Jean Santé. To the right of the Couloir Pombie-Souzon are the Main and Doigt de Pombie and to the right again the slabs of the Voie Fouquier. The East Face is a very broad, easy ridge which gives the line of the ordinary route. The North Face of the Grand Pic, best approached from the Lac de Bious-Artigues, has as its principal feature the Eperon North de la Pointe de France. The North Face of the Petit Pic, best approached from the Lac de Pombie via the col de Peyreget has as its principal feature the Eperon North running from the lowest point on the face directly to the summit. Between these two magnificent buttresses lies the Cirque d'Ambarradère. The West Face of the Petit Pic is a jumbled series of ridges and is of the least climbing interest.

The first hard routes on the massif were done by Roger Mailly and Robert Ollivier in the 30's when they made their assaults on the two

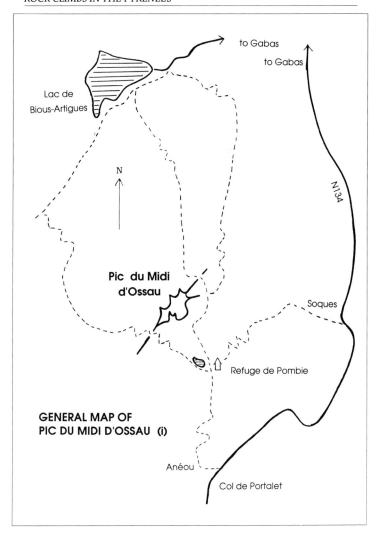

to Gabas

to Gabas

Lac de
Bious-Artigues

N1 34

N

Pic du Midi
d'Ossau

Soques

Refuge de Pombie

**GENERAL MAP OF
PIC DU MIDI D'OSSAU (i)**

Anéou

Col de Portalet

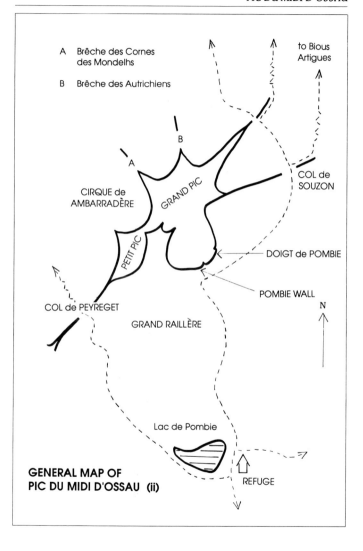

A   Brèche des Cornes
    des Mondelhs

B   Brèche des Autrichiens

to Bious
Artigues

B

A

CIRQUE de
AMBARRADÈRE

GRAND PIC

COL de
SOUZON

PETIT PIC

DOIGT de POMBIE

POMBIE WALL

N

COL de PEYREGET

GRAND RAILLÈRE

Lac de Pombie

**GENERAL MAP OF
PIC DU MIDI D'OSSAU (ii)**

REFUGE

major North buttresses. However, the 50's and 60's proved to be a golden age for high quality lines. Two families featuring prominently, Robert and Jean Ollivier and Jean and Pierre Ravier. These teams opened magnificent lines.

Many climbers have contributed fine routes and the following list of names is in no way comprehensive: Bernard Grenier, Sylvain Sarthou, Patrice de Bellefon, Paul Bouchet, Marcel Bernos, Francis Thomas, Chantal, Raymond Despiau, Roger Mailly and Marcel Jolly.

GRAND PIC   2,884m

Descent

Descent is by the normal route (see route 1). Descend the Rein de Pombie to the east and then an open, slabby, easy-angled couloir just to the left (N) of the East Ridge. This couloir has a 'Portillon' (an iron pole with an arrow) at its head and is found about 20m before the Rein de Pombie steepens and drops down to the East Ridge. From the bottom of the couloir a well-trodden path leads back right to a short chimney, 20m, where care or a rope (for novices) should be used. The path continues to another steepish section, 20m, just above the bottom. This is best descended by first walking 20m right to where holes and pegs will be found in the slabs of the groove. This leads to the grassy ridge above the Col de Souzon.

Eastern Flank
1.   Ordinary Route.   F, with 2 short pitches of 3.   **900m** from the Lac de Pombie.

From the lac follow the path across the Grand Raillère (a large boulder field) to the Col de Souzon. Turn left and go up the ridge to the first rocks. Climb these, 20m, via a groove on the left using man-made holes and wooden pegs. Walk right and follow a path to a short right facing groove. Climb this, 20m and then follow a path diagonally right which leads to easy-angled slabs sloping to the left. These slabs lead to the Rein de Pombie which in turn leads to the summit.

2.   The East Buttress.   AD.   350m.
1st Ascent: 1st December 1957 - Mme. Paullette Dandu, J.Fayet, Robert Ollivier and Jean Ravier.

This route is really a harder alternative to the ordinary route as escape

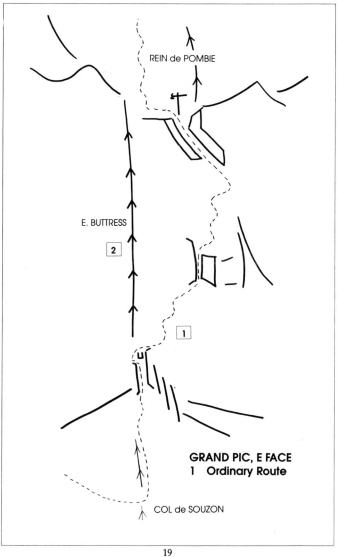

REIN de POMBIE

E. BUTTRESS

2

1

GRAND PIC, E FACE
1   **Ordinary Route**

COL de SOUZON

is possible at many points. Interesting and a very fine winter route.

Start. 10m to the left of the first groove of the ordinary route at a green wall.

Follow the poorly defined arête by the best line, many alternatives being available, the last pitch being up a magnificent black slab giving airy views to the south. A small col leads to the Rein de Pombie.

3. The East Face, the Voie Fouquier. D. 450m. *
1st Ascent: 7th September 1968 - M. and Mme. Fouquier with the guide Jean Louis Pérès.

To the left of the East Ridge is the East Couloir and to the left again a large sweep of slabs which eventually merge into the wall above the Doigt de Pombie. The route climbs the centre of these slabs passing through a steep orange wall at half height, well seen from the path.

Start. At broken white ledges to the right of a small snow field directly below the slabs.

Traverse the ledges to a large V-groove running back right and up to steep rock. Turn this steep barrier on the right and so gain the slabs proper. Climb the compact slabs in 3 excellent pitches, 4c, first slightly left and then back right to good climbing on easier ground. Continue in a direct line to the orange wall. Go through the wall, 4c, and continue easily to terraces at the foot of the final steep section. Several exits are now possible up to the Rein de Pombie.

1) Traverse right and climb out via the East Couloir.
2) Exit via a huge chimney leading left, 5a, on doubtful rock.
3) Climb around the steep arête on the left and then any of the couloirs seen above and to the left.

Northern Flank
Routes on this flank may be approached from the Lac de Pombie via the Col de Souzon or better from Gabas and the Lac de Bious-Artigues. A good path leaves from half-way along the Lac de Bious-Artigues, keeps to the right of the Arête des Mondelhs and enters a grassy amphitheatre above the woods. The path continues on the left to the Brèch de Mondelhs and eventually the Col de Souzon, while on the right will be seen the Les Cornes des Mondelhs ridge. A bay to the left of this ridge leads to the North Face with the Brèche des Autrichiens

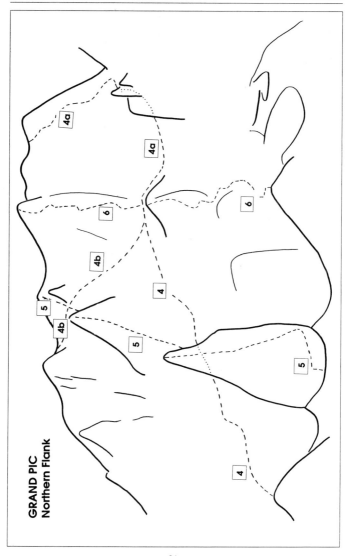

GRAND PIC
Northern Flank

on the left and the Brèche des Cornes des Mondelhs on the right. Good bivouac sites are available in this bay and the wall may be contemplated in the evening whilst surrounded by marmots, isas, weasels and eagles.

4.   The North Face and Fourche.   AD+   650m.   **
1st Ascent: July 1896 - D'Astory, Henri Brulle, Célestin Passet and François Salles.

The route takes a magnificent rising traverse across the North Face, behind the gendarme of the Direct, over the Cirque de l'Ambarradère as far as the Fourche and then a couloir back left to the summit.

Start.   At the Brèche des Autrichiens.

Climb a wall and open chimney to gain easy terraces. Traverse right and climb another chimney to gain an easy couloir which leads to the brèche between the wall and a huge gendarme. From the brèche go up left using the flank of the buttress for 50m, cross the couloir on the right then climb diagonally rightwards to reach a terrace in the middle of the north-west arête of the Pointe de France.

From this point two alternatives are available.

a)   <u>La Fourche.   AD.</u>

Continue the traverse by descending a short groove to a broad terrace which leads across above the Cirque d'Ambarradère and which has the magnificent North-West Face rising on its left. The terrace leads to a long gully, normally containing snow. Climb the wall on the right by its left-hand side (4a) to gain the ridge. Continue along the ridge in magnificent position heading for the Fourche. Before reaching it, climb leftwards up huge slabs (pitons) for three pitches (steps of 4a/4b) before arriving at a good crack on the left. Climb this for two pitches (4a) to a vast couloir/amphitheatre which eventually leads to the summit.

b)   <u>Via the Brèche des Deux Gendarmes.   AD-.</u>

Turn left and go easily up to a small brèche in an arête, after passing beneath a huge chimney which falls from the summit. From this brèche, the Brèche des Deux Gendarmes, cross another small arête behind which is a couloir leading to the Rein de Pombie.

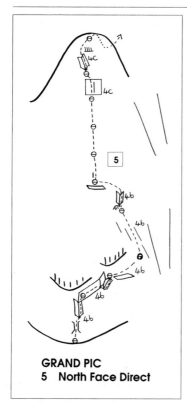

GRAND PIC
5   North Face Direct

5.   North Face Direct.   D. 700m.

1st Ascent: 20th July 1961 - Jean and Pierre Ravier, Jacques Soubis.

Very much a mountaineering route and not really a 'direct.' The difficulties are concentrated on the initial impressive gendarme.

Start. Directly below the summit of the gendarme at a small snow field.

1) 40m. 4b. Climb a steep, broken series of walls and grooves to gain a ramp which leads off to the right.

2, 3) 80m. 4b. Follow the ramp to the right, around the arête and almost into the couloir which bounds the gendarme on the right.

4) 40m. 4b. Climb compact white rock to belay in a niche at the foot of a dièdre.

5) 35m. 4b. Climb the dièdre and traverse left to a platform on the arête in the centre of the buttress.

6) 4c. 7, 8) 120m. Climb a crack above the wall - difficult to start - then continue easily to a wall just below the top of the gendarme.

9) 4c. 10) 4c. 60m. Climb a crack in a black wall and gain a small dièdre on the left. Pass to the left of a grey overhanging wall then come back to the right and hence the gendarme summit.

One is now one-third of the way up, but the remainder may be done quickly and pleasantly.

From the brèche, climb the right side of the buttress for 100m, come back left to the centre and then continue by the best line to the Rein de Pombie.

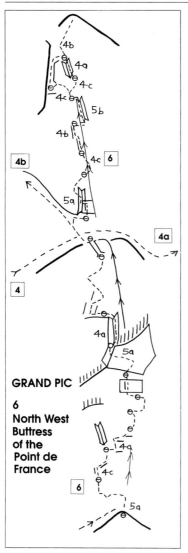

6. North West Buttress of the Pointe de France.
TD. 650m. ***

1st Ascent (lower half): July 1960 - Jean Gardieu, Sylvain Sarthou, Robert and Jean Ollivier .
(Upper half): 24th July 1938 - Roger Mailly and Robert Ollivier.

A magnificent route in a magnificent setting; one of the longest and best on the Pic. As described the route is slightly different from that of the first ascent which made greater use of chimneys. It follows a line just to the left of the buttress axis in the lower half, cutting from right to left just below a prominent overhanging yellow wall, well seen from the lower pitches. The upper half follows the line of the arête.

Start. At the Brèche des Cornes de Mondelhs.

1) 35m. 5a. Climb a difficult wall for 5m and then traverse 25m left before going up to a good belay on a small rib.

2) 40m. 4c. The steep crack behind the belay leads to another which slants diagonally right, arriving eventually at a small bay at the foot of a prominent dièdre.

3) 30m. 4a. Go diagonally right by the easiest line to gain the crest of the buttress.

4, 5) Easy pitches or carry coils slightly on the right, aiming at a prominent, overhanging, yellow wall high on the buttress.

6) 25m. A crack in a steep wall leads to a sloping ledge below a fine slab, beneath the yellow wall.

7) 40m. 5a. Climb the slab diagonally from right to left, in good position, to belay at the foot of a dièdre.

8) 25m. 4a. Good climbing up the dièdre leads to a terrace on the left.

9) Climb the slabs on the left and then *either* regain the crest of the buttress and climb it to the traverse at half height, *or* (more easily) carry coils in the same line until a chimney allows the traverse to be reached.

The upper section of the route is now well seen. It starts just above the foot of the buttress at a cracked wall with dièdres up on its left. (Best approached from the left.)

10) 40m. 5a. Climb the wall and gain the dièdre on the left. After a few metres go round the left arête and climb steeply to a small belay on the narrow arête.

11) 40m. 4c. Climb the sharp arête, slightly on the right to a good belay on its left.

12) 40m. 4b. Climb the left-hand side of the arête via a system of cracks to a ledge in the centre of the arête.

13) 20m. 5b. The Fissure Ollivier. At the right end of the ledge is a very steep dièdre crack. (Good views down the NW Face from here!) Climb the crack or more easily the left-hand wall to a good ledge on the left.

From here, *either*

14) 4c. Climb the wall for a few metres and then traverse left to the base of a huge chimney full of chockstones.

15) 4b. Climb the chimney (strenuous) exiting on the right

or 14a) 4c. Climb the wall and continue in the same line to gain a dièdre around to the right.

15a) 4a. Climb the dièdre.

16) 40m. 4b. Climb the wall on the right via a small ramp slanting up left. Continue to the summit slabs.

Southern Flank

This side of the mountain contains the highest concentration of hard rock climbs. Virtually all the routes are excellent, particularly those on the Pombie Wall. They are long, and though it is not necessary to continue to the summit, the descent from some areas can be a little tricky on the first occasion.

Descents
Pointe Jean Santé

Descend easily on the north side to the Brèche Jean Santé. Continue a further 40m to the Couloir Pombie-Peyreget. This is the second couloir encountered. Descend the couloir by abseil (4) and path to grassy terrain which leads rightwards to the Grande Raillière.

Pombie Wall

I. Routes ending on the 'Vires Inferieures.' (R9)
These 'lower ledges' may be descended without problem but with care.

II. Routes ending in the 'cirque gris.'
From the 'grey amphitheatre' either descend route (R8) (the Voie des Vires), a little complicated, or continue to the Pentagone. From the brèche on its left (W), scramble a few metres left (W) to gain a ledge system on the right (N) side of the Pointe Jean Santé. Climb these for about 25m to reach an easy groove which slants down to the Brèche Jean Santé and the Couloir Pombie-Peyreget.

III. Routes ending on the Aiguillette Jolly.
First gain the Pentagone by a), b) or c) and then continue as for II.

   a) Step across the gap onto the main wall (4c) and climb (difficult for a few metres only) to the second summit of the Aiguillette and then traverse left to the Pentagone.

   b) Descend into the gap, move left (N) and climb the wall (4a) to reach an abseil ledge. Either abseil into the 'cirque gris' or continue as for a).

   c) From the gap, abseil a few metres to an easy ledge which leads to the cirque. Difficult to find.

Main de Pombie

Abseil (2) into the brèche between the Doigt and the main wall, descend as for the Doigt.

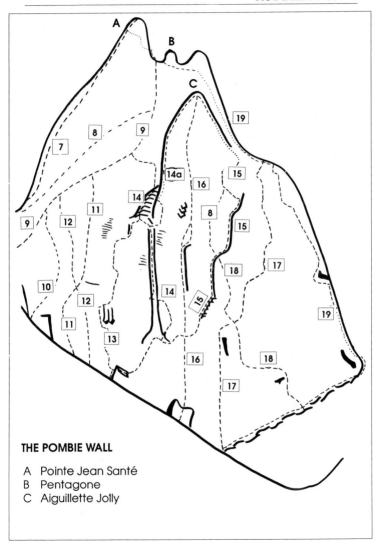

THE POMBIE WALL

A Pointe Jean Santé
B Pentagone
C Aiguillette Jolly

Doigt de Pombie
Either descend the ordinary route or climb the main wall to the Rein de Pombie.

The following three routes give mountaineering-type routes of no great difficulty and which do not really encroach onto the Pombie Wall, but do give access to the Pointe Jean Santé.

7. Couloir Pombie-Peyreget. AD+ 200m.
1st Ascent: 9th August 1942 - Charpentier, Grenier and Jolly.

Start. Walk up the Grande Raillière to a break in the wall (snow frequently) which allows progress to a grassy terrain beneath the couloir.
   Climb the short wall leading to a ledge which runs up into the couloir. Follow the ledge and continuation groove (4b) to where the couloir becomes overhanging. Come out right and climb rocks on the right of the couloir (4a) to a good terrace. Make a long airy traverse right and then climb directly until a crack on the left (4a) leads to easier climbing on the arête. Take the easiest line to the summit.

8. Voie des Vires. AD- 200m.
1st Ascent: 30th July 1933 - Cames, Cazalet, Chicher and Ollivier.

The first route on the wall.

Start. As for the previous route at the short wall below the Couloir Pombie-Peyreget.
   Do not climb the wall but go diagonally right by a series of short walls and sloping slabs to the 'cirque gris' of Pentagone. The route undulates somewhat.
   From the cirque continue to the brèche on the left (W) of the Pentagone, the last 15m best approached by an excursion to the right. Turn left and reach the summit using ledges on the north side of the Pointe.

9. Voie des Vires Infèrieures (Virettes). AD. 200m.
1st Ascent: 29th September 1960 -J.P.Besson and Jean Ollivier.

Start. 50m before the point at which the previous routesleavethe Grande Raillière.
   Follow the ramp, past a cave before descending a little to gain a

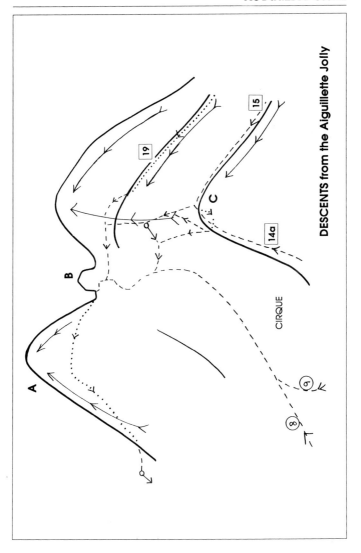

DESCENTS from the Aiguillette Jolly

couloir. Continue rightwards, after descending a little, up short walls. A short crack (4b) and wall give access to a large platform. Traverse right again until a buttress leads to the 'cirque gris.'

10. Voie Mailly. TD- 200m. **
1st Ascent: 18th August 1935 - J.Arruyer, G.Busquet, F.Cazalet, R.Mailly and J.Santé.

Short, easy to follow, pleasant climbing with one well-protected hard move and simple descent; all the attributes of a popular route after a late start.

Start.   100m below the ramp of R9, just to the left of an obvious upside down L-shaped overhang, at a left facing break.

1) 35m. 4b. Climb the cracked slab and then the wall of the short chimney to ledges on the right.

2) 40m. 4b. Continue easily diagonally right until a steep crack leads to more ledges. From here the Grande Dièdre is accessible to the right, however instead;

3) 20m. 4a. Climb diagonally left to the base of a fine dièdre, the start of which contains a jammed flake.

4) 35m. 5b. Take the right-hand side of the flake and continue up the dièdre to a terrace below a long chimney, dièdre.

5) 40m. 4b. Nice climbing up the dièdre and its right-hand wall leads to a belay on the left below another jammed flake.

6) 20m. 4b. Overcome the flake and continue to the Voie des Vires Infèrieures.

11. The Flip Matinal. TD+ 200m. *
1st Ascent: August 1978 - Tony Bedel, Michel Fabbro and Bruno Prat.

A short difficult route with some aid, on excellent rock but with escape possible at mid-height.

Start.   About 80m lower than R10 at a good looking dièdre with a compact slab on its left. The route climbs the dièdre, a crack on the left and then uses aid to reach a crack on the right which leads to easy terraces at mid-height. Sustained climbing up the compact overlapping slabs to the right of R12 enables the descent traverse of R9 to be reached.

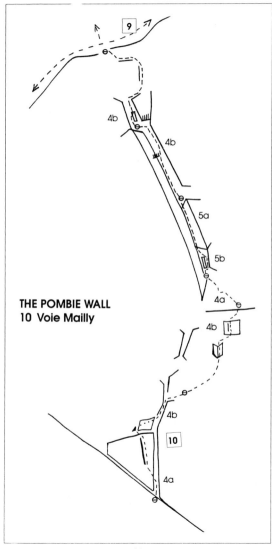

THE POMBIE WALL
10 Voie Mailly

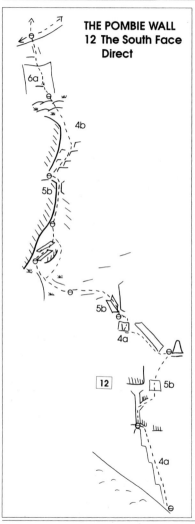

THE POMBIE WALL
12 The South Face
Direct

12. The South Face Direct. TD+ 400m (To the Jean Santé). **
1st Ascent: 31st May, 1st June 1959 - Bernard Grenier and Jean Ravier.

A long excellent route marred by having several escapes and some aid in the Grande Dièdre, though the route does go free.

Start. At a very prominent ramp leading to an overhang.

Climb the ramp, 4a, go around the right of the overhang and continue to a block gendarme, 5b. Climb diagonally left to easy terraces, cross R11 and continue to the Grande Dièdre. This is gained slightly from the left and then climbed in three pitches to an exit left via blocks and a final difficult finger crack. From here it is possible to descend or continue to the Pointe Jean Santé after crossing R8.

Pic du Midi d'Ossau, The Pombie Wall from the lake
Photo: I. Jones

Pic du Midi d'Ossau, South Pillar. View down the hard section. Climber: Nando Guzman Photo: J.Armesta

The Espelon Este, Ordesa. The Rabadà-Navarro takes the large overhangs and then the diedre slightly on the right of the final arête. Photo: N.McEvett

13. Voie des Surplombs. TD. 200m. **
1st Ascent: August 1971 - Jean Brossard, Roland Ducournau and Robert Mizrahi

Start. 100m above the ramp which leads to the couloir Pombie-Souzon at a left facing broken groove, just to the left of the Jolly chimney. This groove gives easy access to a very regular slab which slants down to the right and which is taken by the Sud-Est.

1) 30m. 4a. Climb the groove for 15m and then go diagonally left to a short crack which leads to a good stance below an A-shaped overhang.

2) 30m. 4c. The smooth wall on the left is used to gain a dièdre which slants to the right and leads to another good stance beneath the overhang.

3) 30m. 4c. Traverse left for 10m and climb a superb dièdre to a platform on the right.

4) 40m. 4a. Straight up by the easiest line to a belay below a very steep section.

5) 40m. 4a. Avoid the steep section by climbing on the left until a short traverse right leads to a fierce looking chimney.

6) 40m. 5a. Climb direct and so gain the cirque gris.

14. Voie Jolly. TD. 250m to easy ground. ***
1st Ascent: 31st August 1946 - M.Jolly, P.Limargues and M. & J.Arnautou.

An excellent route, particularly when combined with the Super Jolly.

Start. As for R13.

1) 30m. 4a. Climb the groove to the tree root covered slab.

2) 40m. 4c. Descend the slab and cross to easier broken rock on the right. Climb up to a pedestal and belay on a ledge down to the right.

3) 30m. 4a. Climb the pleasant chimney directly above the ledge and then go diagonally left up a line of ribs.

4) 45m. 4c. Continue in the same line to a shoulder which allows a traverse left into the main chimney. It is best to traverse at a high level.

5, 6, 7) 4c. with a few 5b steps. Superb climbing up dièdres and cracks to easy ground and a stepped tongue which runs down from the cirque gris.

8, 9) Easily left to the arête of the tongue, up this until it is possible to traverse left below steep walls.

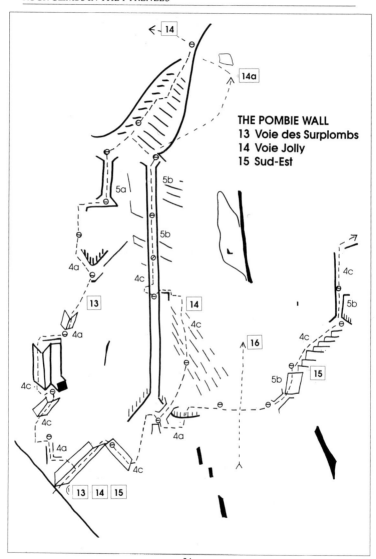

THE POMBIE WALL
13 Voie des Surplombs
14 Voie Jolly
15 Sud-Est

10) Traverse left until easy ground is reached leading back right above the steep walls to the cirque.

Continue to the Pentagone and hence the descent.

14a.   The Super Jolly.   TD-   200m.   *
1st Ascent: 17th July 1970 - Patrick Lamarque and Jean-Louis Pérès.

A magnificent extension to routes finishing in the 'cirque gris.'

Start.   in the 'cirque gris.'

Climb without great difficulty to a large yellow wall high on the right. Traverse left under the wall, go round the arête to a good crack and climb it (5a). Continue to a dièdre which leads (4c) to a good belay platform below a very steep wall. Climb the wall (5a) to a traverse left around ribs which leads to a belay on the arête. Follow the arête to the summit.

15.   The Sud-Est.   TD-   400m.   *** (see diagram p38)
1st Ascent: 8th May 1953 - André Armengaud and Jean Ravier.

The so called 'classical route.' A tremendous outing; easily the most repeated; not to be missed.

The climb traverses across the wall to gain the 'grande dièdre,' follows this and then returns along the arête to the summit of the Aiguillette Jolly.

Start.   As for R13.

1, 2)   As for R14.

3) 30m. 4a. Traverse right and go through the bulge at a break to reach easy ledges running right.

4) 35m. Traverse easily right to a wide crack.

5) 30m. 5a. Climb the crack and smooth slab to a belay on the right.

6) 25m. 4b. The 'escaliers gris' ('grey stairs' - well seen from the ground) lead to the foot of a fine dièdre.

7) 30m. 5a. 8) 25m. 4c. Climb the dièdre to a vast terrace.

9, 10) 80m. 4b. From the right-hand end of the terrace climb the obvious dièdre by the easiest line, sometimes the right-hand arête, to a good platform.

11) 25m. 4b. Climb the groove and cracks above to a jammed block in the left wall and use this to traverse round the corner to a smooth ledge system.

12) 25m. 4c. Go diagonally left up the ledges to a short, wide crack

in a steep wall and climb it to a sloping stance.

13) 25m. 5a. Continue up the crack for a short way to a good ledge which leads right to the arête where a delicate wall gives access to easy ground in a vast couloir.

14, 15) 80m. 4a. Climb the chimney up on the left and follow it and the left arête to the summit of the Aiguillette Jolly.

16. The Sud-Est Direct. ED- 350m. ***
!st Ascent: 2-4th May 1964 - Paul Bouchet and Jean and Pierre Ravier.

A magnificent and difficult route. It has several aid sections but has been climbed free.

Start. Half-way between the ordinary route and the lowest point of the wall, at two large flakes.

Climb between the flakes and continue via a crack leaning to the left and a chimney leaning to the right to the easy traverse of the Sud-Est, pitch 4. Continue directly for two pitches to gain a magnificent dièdre which is climbed in three pitches. Descend a little to the right to gain a large couloir which goes to the right of three stepped overhangs.

Follow the couloir for one pitch to the level of a yellow wall, traverse left to a crack, climb it and then come back right to dièdres which lead to less steep ground. Continue direct to the summit of the Aiguillette Jolly.

17. The Voie Thomas. ED- 400m. **
1st Ascent: June 1974 - Henri Santam, Dominique Séguier, Francis Thomas and Claude Trey.

A similar route to the previous one. It starts a few metres to the left of the ramp which leads to the Couloir Pombie-Souzon and follows an obvious line of dièdres and cracks.

18. The East Face Direct. ED- 400m.
1st Ascent: July 1982 - Léopold Lareng, Francis Ourou, Gérard Pécune and Christian Sébie.

The route follows a line of cracks on superb rock, with several A2 sections in its lower half.

19. The East Buttress. TD. 400m. **
1st Ascent: 4, 5th July 1955 - Jean and Pierre Ravier.

A first class route in a tremendous position. It starts in the bay at the foot of the Couloir Pombie-Souzon, climbs the left-hand side of the buttress to the shoulder, traverses left and finishes up the couloir leading to the small col on the right of the second summit of the Aiguillette Jolly.

Start. From the lowest point of the Pombie Wall, walk up the Grande Raillère for 50m and climb the ramp which leads to the Couloir Pombie-Souzon. The route starts at a point to the right of the arête, where the overhang is at its smallest.

1) 40m. 5a. Climb the small overhang, fingery, and then go diagonally right along a series of ramps.

2) 40m. 5a. Gain the leftmost of two fine looking dièdres via a small overhang and climb it to a small belay in good position.

3) 30m. 5b. Go up the cracked wall to the roof and then traverse down to the left in order to go around the roof to belay on a broken ledge.

4) 40m. 4a. Continue left for a few metres until it is possible to come back right to easier ground leading to the crest of the buttress.

5) 40m. 4b. Climb the buttress using a chimney to belay at the foot of a steep, wide crack.

6) 40m. 4c. Climb directly to a very good ledge below a steep wall.

7) 30m. 5c. Go diagonally left across the wall to a crack and climb it to a very small ledge.

8) 4c. A few metres of climbing up the wall allows easier ground to be reached on the shoulder.

9, 10) Two easy pitches diagonally left to a huge couloir with a fine dièdre in its left-hand corner. This is the leftmost couloir of several seen high above the shoulder.

11) 40m. 5a. Climb the dièdre for 15m until a delicate exit right may be made and then go up to another dièdre on the right.

12) 40m. 5a. Climb the dièdre for 15m until it is possible to move left over a small overhang. Continue steeply by the line of least resistance to the summit arête.

Go easily rightwards to the Pentagone and the descent.

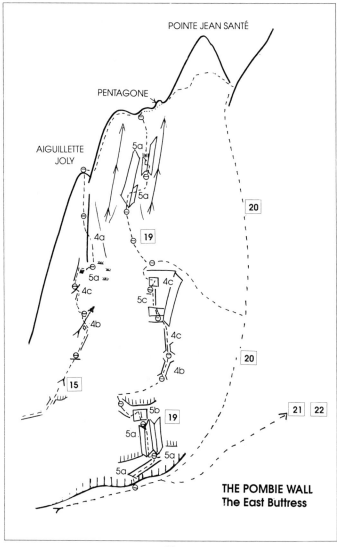

POINTE JEAN SANTÉ

PENTAGONE

AIGUILLETTE JOLY

5a

5a

20

4a

19

5a

4c

4b

4c

5c

4c

4b

15

5b

19

5a

5a

5a

21 22

THE POMBIE WALL
The East Buttress

20.   Couloir Pombie-Souzon.   D+   350m.
1st Ascent: 26th August 1928 - Marcel Cames, Roger Cazabonne and Jean Santé.

An early route, not often repeated because of stone fall risk, but in very good position. It gives a very good mixed route in spring using the connection to the shoulder of the East Buttress.

✳   ✳   ✳

LE DOIGT ET MAIN DE POMBIE
These two subsidiary points are separated from the Pombie Wall by the Couloir Pombie-Souzon and give excellent climbing. Although the hard climbing is not overlong, the 200m scramble to the base of the routes, the good position and the possibilities of a continuation above combine to give a big route feel to the climbing.

21.   Le Main de Pombie, Y. Cracks.   TD.   250m.   **
1st Ascent: September 1967 - Marcel Bernos, Jaques Bladé and Yves Darcourt.

Start.   Follow the ramp to the bay at the foot of the Couloir Pombie-Souzon as for R19, climb the slabs on the right to an easy broken terrace at the foot of the wall. At the extreme left-hand end of the terrace is a dièdre crack at the foot of the Y-shaped feature which leads diagonally left to the summit. The route starts at the foot of the crack.

1) 25m. 4c. Climb the crack, exiting right on to an area of stepped slablets.

2) 45m. 4a. Climb the slablets to belay at the foot of a very steep wall.

3) 40m. 5a. Go around the arête on the right and then climb a series of ribs with a delicate finish left to gain an impressive dièdre.

4) 40m. 5b. The dièdre gives excellent climbing until a short traverse left and a steep crack lead to a good belay.

5) 35m. 4c, 6a/Ao. The steep crack behind the belay leads to an overhanging groove. Climb this with or without the aid to a bay.

6, 7) 100m. 4a. Take the line of least resistance first right and then left to the summit. The climbing becoming progressively easier.

From the col between the summit and the main massif, two abseils lead to easy ground and the col between the Doigt and the main massif.

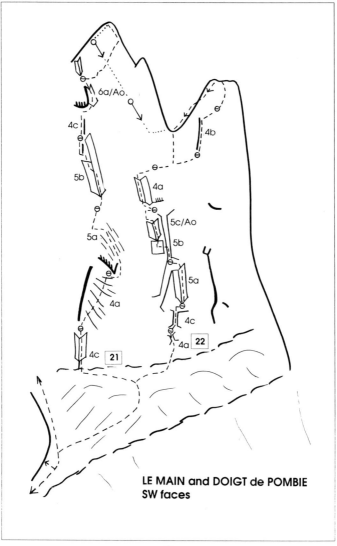

LE MAIN and DOIGT de POMBIE
SW faces

22.   Le Doigt de Pombie, South Face.   TD.   200m.   **
!st Ascent: 7th June 1956 - Jean Ravie, Pierre Ravier and Jacques Soubis.

Start.   As for R21 to the broken terrace. The line of the route is a crack system running from the col between the Doigt and Main to near the right-hand end of the terrace. Start on the right below the cracks.

1) 25m. 4a. Climb a short wall and then a wide crack to a ledge below a chimney.

2) 25m. 4c. Use the chimney to gain a good ledge at the right-hand end of which is a fine dièdre.

3) 40m. 5a. Excellent sustained climbing up the dièdre with an exit left to a belay in a chimney.

4) 35m. 5b, 5c/Ao. Climb the chimney for 10m and then traverse left across the smooth wall for 5m until hard moves upwards bring one to a short overhanging dièdre. Climb this with or without the peg to a good belay a few metres higher.

5) 40m. 4a. A choice of routes lead on to easy ground and the shallow couloir which leads to the col.

Instead of climbing the couloir walk 40m right to a fine-looking crack leading to just left of the summit. Climb this, 4b, and then trend right and finally back left to the top. An easy descent, slightly on the left, leads down to the col.

23.   Le Doigt de Pombie, East Face.   TD-   350m.   *
1st Ascent: 1975 - Henri Beaudéant, Gilbert Bergès, Tony Bedel and Daniel Gillereau.

An excellent climb but escapable at mid-height. The first half follows a line of cracks on the right while the upper half the line of least resistance starting on the left of some reddish slabs.

Start.   At some light-coloured rocks leading to the crack system which splits the steep red wall. Sometimes a small snow field at the base.

1) 30m. 4b. Climb the clear rocks and a short crack to a belay below a second crack leading left.

2) 30m. 4c. Go up the wide crack and continue to a good platform at the foot of the main crack system.

3) 25m. 5b. Above is a leaning crack, layback this or climb the wall on the right and then continue up the groove on the left.

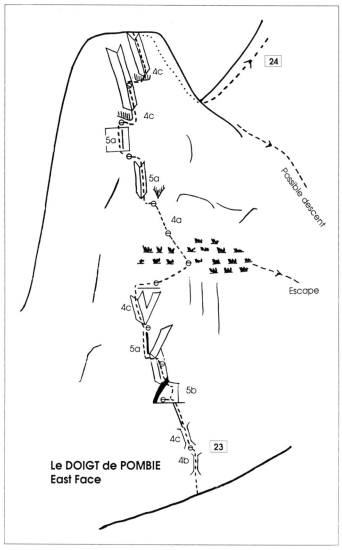

24

4c

4c

5a

5a

4a

Escape

Possible descent

4c

5a

5b

4c

23

4b

**Le DOIGT de POMBIE
East Face**

4) 25m. 5a. Continue in the same line until it is possible to traverse left around the arête to another crack which leads to a good ledge.

5) 35m. 4c. Continue slightly on the left up some nice dièdres until it is possible to go rightwards and so gain easy ground.

Escape is now possible to the right.

6,7) 4a. From the top of the easy ground go diagonally left up slabs aiming generally for the summit until one arrives at the foot of a small, dark, triangular overhang.

8) 25m. 5a. Go round the left of the overhang and up a nice corner.

9) 35m. 5a. Climb easily up to the left to a steep wall and climb this via a crack to a good platform below steep rock.

10) 35m. 4c. Descend to the right to a groove and go up this to an awkward belay in very impressive surroundings.

11) 40m. 4c. Cross to the right-hand side of the groove and go over a small yellow overhang to another groove around the right of an arête. This leads without difficulty to the summit.

24.   La Rein via la Doigt.   AD-   500m.   *
1st Ascent: 1940 - René Ballini and Jean Trézière.

An excellent mountaineering route.

Start.   As for the Voie Fouquier. Pass under this route and climb the couloir to the brèche between the Doigt and the main wall. The sides of the couloir give pleasant climbing and allow an overhang at the top to be turned by a delicate wall, 4a. After topping the Doigt, slightly from the right, and returning to the brèche, the climb is resumed by attacking the main wall. Climb slightly right for 80 metres and then come back left. Many ways are possible and it may be found necessary to break through a steep rib on the left before reaching the exit couloirs and the Rein de Pombie. The second half gives a very natural and pleasing finish to routes 21, 22 and 23.

The south buttress of the Grand Pic is a very prominent feature of the view from the Pombie hut, dominating the left-hand skyline.

24a.   Grand Pic, South Pillar.   MD Sup.   400m.   ***
1st Ascent: 5/6th July 1959 - P. de Bellephon, R.Despiau, B.Grenier and J.Ravier.

An excellent but shortish route with a long approach. The rock is good, the exposure superb and the finish is on the summit.

The steep and frequently overhanging South Pillar is split by a deep chimney which drops almost to the South Cirque. The route starts slightly to the left of the line of this chimney and climbs a beautiful series of sustained dièdres to the left of it before traversing right at the top to easy ground on the South East Face. First an aid route, it has now been done free but most parties do a mixture. At 5b/5c only a handful of Ao steps are required.

Start. From the Lac de Pombie follow the path towards the Col de Peyreget and then skirt the Grande Raillère by its western edge to gain the South Cirque.

1, 2) 70m. Climb easy rock slightly leftwards to gain a good platform below a right facing corner.

3) 40m. Follow the corner with one 5a move at mid-height to another platform.

4) 25m. 4a. Another corner.

(Pitches 3) and 4) may be avoided by a groove around the rib on the left but this is harder and less pleasant.)

Above is a square-cut dièdre with a crack in the right wall, tantalisingly far from the corner.

5) 40m. Ao. 5c. The dièdre to mid-height and then a two metre traverse right to a crack which leads to a small block platform.

6) 50m. Ao. 5c. This pitch is usually split with an exciting hanging stance. Climb the groove to the overhang and then traverse left for 3m to a groove which leads to a corner. Climb the corner with a short excursion to the right and a crack (possible belay) before regaining the corner and a final exit on the left. Easy ground leads up to the right and a belay on a clean cracked slab.

7) 45m. Ao. 5c. Go round the arête on the right and climb a shallow dièdre before traversing right below an overhanging wall which gives access to a cave and possible belay. This cave is at the top of the aforementioned chimney. Leave the cave by a crack on the right and gain a superb spike and then ledge out on the wall. Good position here. Follow the clean cracks for 8m until a short traverse right leads to a broken block ledge and belay.

This is the end of the major difficulties. 130m. Traverse a few metres right and then climb up to easy ground. Continue up and then left to the arête before following it rightwards to the summit.

※　　※　　※

PETIT PIC   2,807m

Although having a very fine Matterhorn-type appearance, the Petit Pic does not provide as much rock climbing interest as the Grand Pic, However, the North Buttress is a classic which at one time was considered the hardest route in the area, and if done totally free is still very demanding.

Descent

This follows the west flank of the Peyreget ridge and provides no problems.

From the summit descend about 40m to the SE (in the direction of the Lac de Pombie) to a platform and abseil point above a 35m wall. After the abseil an open couloir leads down leftwards to the Peyreget ridge. Follow this, at first on the left and then easily down to the right along paths at a comfortable angle. A path is met which traverses a long way leftwards between outcrops arriving eventually at the Col de Peyreget.

25.   North Buttress.   TD.   500m.   ***

The buttress was climbed by a variety of variations between 1963 and 1967 through the efforts of Phillipe Sol, Claude Valleau, Marcel Bernos, Paul Bouchet, Bernard Grenier and Jean and Pierre Ravier.

The route described is the best and the accepted 'direct' line. An excellent route. It follows a line of dièdres on the right of the initial section and then turns the middle of the steepest section by an excursion to the left.

Approach from the Lac de Pombie via the Col de Peyreget.

Start.   30m above and to the right of the lowest point of the buttress at some easy slabs leading to the crest of the buttress.

1, 2, 3) Climb up to the crest of the buttress and then its right-hand side to gain the foot of a fine dièdre which slants back to the crest.

4, 5) 4b. Climb the dièdre to arrive at a small shoulder where the arête steepens.

6) 35m. 5a. Use a crack on the right-hand side of the arête to gain a ledge system. Continue left along the ledge for a further 30m passing a line of pitons which lead back to the arête and which are to be ignored.

7) 40m. 5c. Climb a corner for 15m, go over a small overhang on the right to gain a ledge and continue up a line of shallow grooves to

a good belay on a long ledge. An excellent pitch.

8) 40m. 5b. Go to the right-hand end of the rising ledge and climb a steep, smooth wall to a belay on the right of the arête.

9) 50m. 4c. Climb the cracked blocks behind the belay, continue up a crack (6a, Ao), and belay on a good ledge on the left of the arête.

10) 40m. 4c. A square-cut groove soon leads to easier ground on the arête and hence the shoulder of the Pic.

Carry coils to near the foot of the final tower and then take an airy traverse leftwards towards the 'Fourche.'

11) 40m. 4b. 50m before the 'Fourche,' climb a broad line of weakness over short walls to gain a couloir on the left.

12) Climb the couloir to the summit.

26. TD. The original route up the North Buttress climbed its NE flank and it is possible to continue traversing left after pitch 6 of R25 to gain a line of chimneys and cracks which form its upper part.

27. TD- Several lines enter from the right to join R25 after pitch 8, the best being the 'Voie des Dalles.' This starts in the centre of the NW Face and takes the easiest line to reach the huge slabs to the right of the steepest part of the North Buttress. Superb traversing pitches on good rock now lead to the arête.

28. West Face. D- 350m.
1st Ascent: 3rd July 1934 - François Cazalet, Roger Mailly and Robert Ollivier.

Start. Halfway up the face is a large easy-angled amphitheatre. Gain this via a huge couloir from the foot of the face or by traversing in from the 'Flammes des Pierre' arête.

From the top of the amphitheatre follow a groove which eventually becomes a chimney. After an excursion into the mountain itself arrive at a superb airy platform. Continue up a dièdre to the summit, 4 pitches, 4b.

29. Arête de Peyreget. AD- 500m.
1st Ascent: 1858 - Jean Biraben with 2 clients.

Start. At the Col de Peyreget.

Walk up the left (W) side of the ridge on grass and gain the second of two brèches, by a red gendarme. Descend slightly to the right using a couloir which drops down towards the Grande Raillère and then follow a path up the right flank of the ridge to the summit cone. A chimney is used (and now a rope) to gain the summit slope.

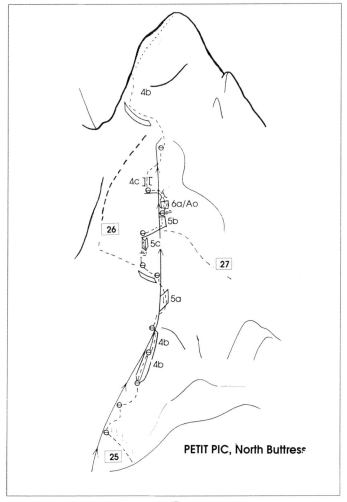

PETIT PIC, North Buttress

ORDESA

"Civilisation has stretched out its hand, changed it all, and though those who know the old days are somewhat sad that the old order has changed, yielding place to new yet the new order is good and the land of the great woods, lakes, mountains and rushing rivers is still mysterious enough to please anyone who has eyes to see, and can understand."

Norman Collie

The Ordesa valley is an area of outstanding natural beauty, the equal of any in Europe. Mountains, waterfalls, towering cliffs, forests and wildlife all contribute to the ambience. The combination of Ordesa and Monte Perdido form one of Spain's nine national parks. As such, it is a very popular tourist area providing many interesting outings, varying from simple 3-hour walks to multi-day journeys which include 3,000-metre peaks, glaciers and snow fields, even in summer. The park is 'controlled' and visitors would do well to aquaint themselves with the simple rules made available at the park entrance. The concept of rules is an anathema to the free spirit of the climbing world, however it is possible to state without reservation that the park has been kept completely free of litter and is totally unspoilt. Camping is not permitted but an overnight bivouac is allowed. Long term camping and other accommodation is available in Torla.

Many books have been written about the detailed structure of the area, but from the climber's point of view it is sufficient to know that from the car park a 1¹/₂-hour walk through forests leads to 400m sandstone cliffs of almost fairytale appearance above which grassy terraces lead to 200m limestone headwalls, as yet unclimbed. It is usual to bivouac the night before climbing. Some thought should be given to the availability of water during summer and autumn.

The three principal climbing areas are the Tozal del Mallo, a fin-shaped peak seen immediately upon entering the valley; the Gallinero, which dominates the car park and the Fraucata which faces west and half blocks the head of the valley. These walls, without being mountains, are generally considered to be too much for an 'escuela.'

The climbing rock is a tan-coloured hard sandstone, generally sound and with good protection but also with the occasional loose section on some routes. Good quality technical moves are the order of the day, but the majority of the routes are undertaken because of

Above: The Gallinero, Ordesa Canyon. Photo: J.Armesta

From the fourth belay of 'La Murciana', Riglos. The 'vertical potato field' proves to have incredible rock and holds! Climbers: D.Reade, J.Armesta, D.L.Walker, F.Guzman. Photo: A.Harman

Ordesa Canyon Photo: D.L. Walker

the appeal of the lines. They have a big feel to them and retreat may sometimes be difficult because of the large overhangs.

Climbing is possible all year round as the cliffs face south or west. Only certain routes are available in spring because of melting snow from the terraces above and care is needed in winter because of storms due to the mountain environment.

The opening of a new route in the valley has always been seen as a major event. 1957 saw the first route on the South Face of the Tozal by a party led by Jean Ravier, followed in 1960 by another major line, the Franco-Espanola - a combination of routes by two parties.

Rabadá and Navarro did several routes, but their ascent of the East Buttress of the Gallinero in 1961 was a major *tour de Force* over three days. During the first ascent it was felt necessary to leave a fixed rope down the large overhang in the case of retreat.

The Mondarruego Wall overlooking Torla was climbed in 1964 but is very rarely repeated. The 'open-book' section of the Gallinero had to wait until 1975 before being breached by Despiau and Battaia. La Fraucata, previously known as 'El Castillo Refulgente,' the Shining Castle, saw its first route in 1966, done by Anglada and Cerda, who along with Civis produced other fine routes in the canyon. More recently, Jesús Gálvez has done several very good and very hard lines.

Pitch 2 of Murciana (Via Alberto Rabadá), Riglos Climber: D. Reade
Photo: A. Harman   49

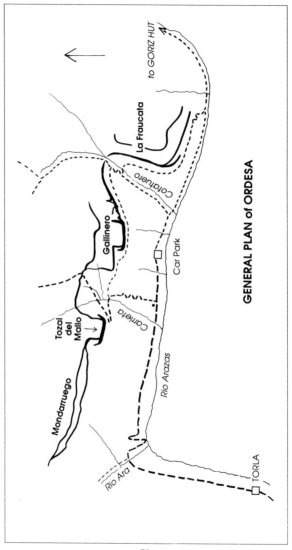

GENERAL PLAN of ORDESA

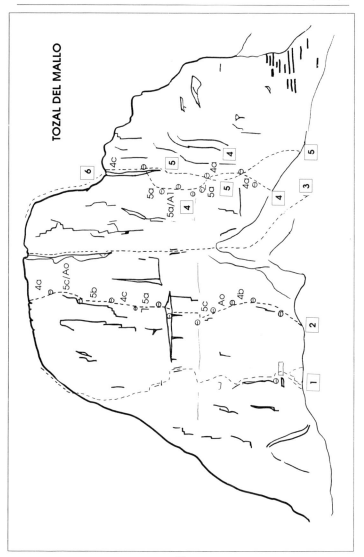

TOZAL DEL MALLO

Descents
These are all without problem.

Tozal del Mallo
Follow the rim of the Circo de Salarons to the right (East) until one meets the main path which descends from the high plateau via the clavijas (iron pegs) to the car park down the Barranco Carrieta.

Gallinero
Either follow the plateau to the right (East) to meet the main path from the Brecha de Rolando and descend this via the clavijas de Cotatuero alongside the waterfall *or*, descend the huge couloir 200m to the right (East) of the 'Espolon de la Primavera' (Spring Buttress) which bounds the eastern extremity of the 'open book' section. This is a scramble where care is required, the last 50m of which is avoided by a detour to the right (West) and tree abseil.

La Fraucata
Traverse left with care across the scree slope, cross the Cotatuero, sometimes difficult (or at least damp) and descend the clavijas.

TOZAL DEL MALLO
This is probably the most popular of the climbing areas as the routes are long and they finish on the top of a spectacular peak, previously known as 'el Retablo del Altar.' (Loosely translated as the Altar Showpiece.) The pitches are usually vertical or gently overhanging but with good belay ledges.

Approach is up the path which leaves the road 500m before the car park, at the information chalet. This path leads to the foot of the wall before slanting up right to the clavijas, just before which the path diverges, the right-hand branch passing underneath the Gallinero on its way to the waterfall of the Cotatuero. The clavijas lead up to a hanging amphitheatre, the Circo des Salarons, scene of some new developments and then on to the Brecha de Rolando.

1.   Brujas.   ED.   425m.   ***
1st Ascent: 27th, 28th, 29th June 1963 - A. Rabadá, E. Navarro and J.J.Diaz.

Long thought to be one of the best and hardest routes in the area,

---

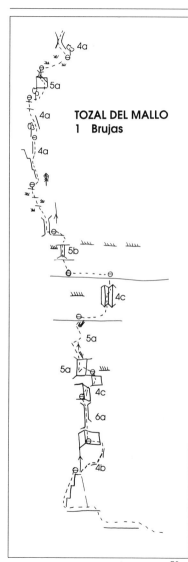

TOZAL DEL MALLO

1   Brujas

certainly a very airy line. It takes a crack system on the left-hand side of the wall as far as the Plaza Cataluña, traverses left to a weakness in the overhangs and then finishes up the line of least resistance on the west wall, using large trees as belays. An excellent logical line on good rock.

Start. At a shattered pillar just to the right of a black streaked wall which has a crack on its left.

1) 25m. Easily up the left-hand side of the pillar to belay on a pedestal.

2) 30m. 4b. Diagonally right up walls to a good ledge with a belay at its left-hand corner.

3) 35m. 6a/Ao. The groove above is very strenuous and leads to a good belay in a corner containing a fine crack.

4) 25m. 4c. Climb the corner using the right-hand wall and then a slab on the right to belay on a good ledge.

5) 45m. 5a. Go up left and then traverse or descend leftwards to a crack which runs up to an arête. Continue for a few metres until it is possible to come back right to a wall. Climb this and exit, on the left-hand side of projecting rock, to a narrow ledge running across the wall.

La Plaza de Cataluña Climbers: J. Armesta F. Guzman
Photo: D.L. Walker

A fine pitch, any equipment dropped at this point will return to the starting point without touching rock. Proven.

6) 45m. 4c. Walk 10m right to dièdres and climb these to the Plaza Cataluña.

7) 30m. Walk left to belay below a square-cut groove.

8) 30m. 5b. Climb the little wall and then the overhanging groove on excellent holds to a belay in a niche up on the left. A nice gritstone exercise.

9) 40m. Step left and climb an easy chimney and then grassy terraces diagonally leftwards. There is a tall isolated tree up on the right.

10) 35m. 4a. An easy broken ramp and pleasant crack leads to another good tree.

11) 25m. 4a. The crack behind the tree and then short walls lead to another tree.

12) 30m. 5a. The slab above can be tricky.

13, 14) 60m. The terrace and open couloir lead to the summit via yet another tree.

2. La Franco-Española. ED 350m. ***
1st Ascent (lower part):19th, 20th September 1960 - P. de Bellephon and S.Sarthou.
(Upper part): 11th, 12th June 1960 - J.M.Anglada and F.Guillamon.

A superbly spectacular route on good rock in its upper half. It starts 50m to the left of the flying buttress at a rightward slanting weakness and climbs directly to the midway terrace, Plaza Cataluña. From here it takes the obvious crack in the centre of the face, complete with overhangs. The better (and tougher) combination uses the first half of Brujas to mid-height.

3. Ravier. MD+ 350m. ***
1st Ascent: 20th-21st April 1957 - N.Blotti, C.Dufourmantelle, C.Jaccoux, M.Kahn and J.Ravier.

Another superb route by the Frenchman from Bordeaux; one of the great classics of Ordesa. Very few ascents in the first ten years and usually then with a bivouac, now a trade route. Logical in line and on excellent rock but rather polished on the crux chimney.

Start. Scramble up to the col formed by the small flying buttress

Looking down Ravier, Ordesa Climbers: D.L. Walker F. Guzman
Photo: J. Armesta

and then up to where the wall steepens, directly below the obvious wide hanging chimney 75m.

1) 30m. 4a. 2) 30m. 4a. 3). 30m. 4b. The easiest line to a stance 10m below the chimney.

4) 20m. 5b. Climb up to the chimney and find a technique to overcome it, belay on the right.

5) 25m. 5a. Go diagonally left and then diagonally right to a fine pedestal.

6) 40m. 4c. A superb pitch up the corner above to a comfortable platform below the final dièdre.

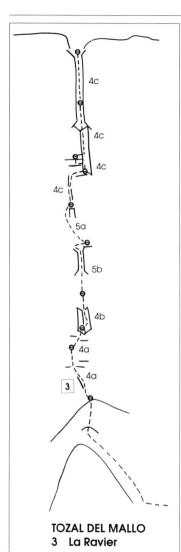

TOZAL DEL MALLO
3   La Ravier

7) 10m. 4c. Climb the corner on the right in order to gain a ledge on the left. Belay up on the left.

8) 45m. 4c. 9) 45m. 4b. Come back right to the corner and continue up the dièdre-chimney to the top.

4.   Anglada-Civis.   MD+ 320m.
1st Ascent: 23rd, 24th June 1968 - J.M.Anglada and E.Civis.

This route makes a rising traverse to start and then takes the easiest and most logical line to the shoulder, with some difficult climbing in the middle section.

5.   Despiau.   MD+   350m.
1st Ascent: 16th-18th May 1969 - R.Boissaire, F.Cassou, and R.Despiau.

A direct on the previous route with harder climbing, more artificial and less pleasing rock.

6.   Gómez-Kahn.   MD- 100m.
1st Ascent:1955 - J.Gómez and M.Kahn.

The natural finish to the previous two routes giving pleasant climbing up the edge of the buttress.

GALLINERO (The Chicken Coop!)

This is a large and very long wall which may best be considered in two halves. El Libro Abierto (the open book) area and the continuation wall to the right which itself has three defined parts, El Tridente, the Espolón Este and La Pared de la Cascada.(The Trident, East Buttress and Waterfall Wall.) Routes on the Libro Abierto take in some very big overhangs, well seen from the car park, while those on the Tridente are short.

Approach is along the path which leaves the eastern end of the car park and which diverges after 500m. The right-hand branch leads to the Goriz Hut and Monte Perdido while the left-hand branch leads up to the waterfall and Clavijas de Cotatuero. When arriving at the river Cotatuero a branch of the path crosses it to the right and leads to the Fraucata, this being its approach. The path ahead eventually diverges, just before the wall is reached, the left-hand branch leading along the foot of the Gallinero before arriving at the Circo de la Carrieta and the Tozal.

7. Princesa Insensible. MD. A2. 490m.
1st Ascent: 15th, 16th June 1983 - J.M.Codina and J.Verdaguer.

A long and difficult route which wends its way between the overhangs at the left-hand end of the wall, taking the most logical line.

Start just to the right of a vegetated section between two large overhangs.

8. La Lluna. MD+ A2. 400m.
1st Ascent: August 1984 - S.Galar, T.Eizmendi and I.Lacalle.

A very direct route with a very big overhang.

9. Sol Negro. MD+ 360m.
1st Ascent: 7th, 8th, 9th June 1977 - C.Desbats, D.Julien, R.Munsch and D.Tollet.

A difficult route, not easy to follow. The large overhang has a fixed hanging rope.

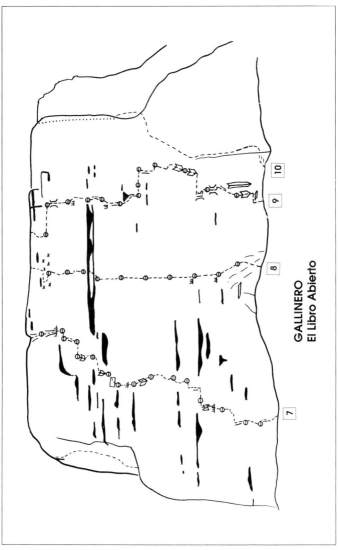

GALLINERO
El Libro Abierto

10.   The Anglada-Cerda.   MD-   375m.   **
1st Ascent: 12th June 1966 - J.M.Anglada and J.Cerda.

An old classic, with escape possible at half-height. The upper half takes the prominent open corner well seen from the east end of the valley.

Start.   To the left of a 100 metre buttress which is well to the left of the upper corner.

   1) 35m. Climb up to ledges and then go around the arête and up to ribs.

   2) 30m. 4b. Climb a small crack, just to the right of a deep crack and belay on the crest of the buttress.

   3) 35m. 4b. Continue to the start of a wide, easy couloir running up right.

   4) 40m. 4a. Climb the couloir to belay at the foot of a square-cut, shallow chimney.

   5) 35m. 5a. Use the two cracks to gain ledges and continue, slightly right, to a good belay.

   6) 45m. 4a. Take the easiest line rightwards in an airy position to gain grass terraces and possible escape.

   7) 30m. 4c. Good climbing up ribs with a final traverse right leads to a platform at the foot of a prominent left facing dièdre.

   8) 35m. 5a. Traverse 3m right and climb a series of cracks to a belay below a projecting overhang.

   9) 10m. 4c. Continue up the steep groove to easy ground.

   10, 11) 80m. Pleasant climbing up the open couloir to the top.

11.   Destino Petrala.   MD.   300m.
1st Ascent: May 1985 - K.Bayona and J.Ruiz.

A good route, but broken in the middle.

12.   Espolón de la Primavera.   MD.   200m.   *
1st Ascent: 16th June 1974 - R.Despiau and J.P.Barokas.

A popular route in good position, though short.

Start.   A large pine at the end of the first pitch is a good marker. The climb starts 20m lower at the left-hand end of a very long approach ledge just to the left of a prominent overhanging chimney

   1) 25m. 4c. Move left from a bush, climb a corner and traverse left

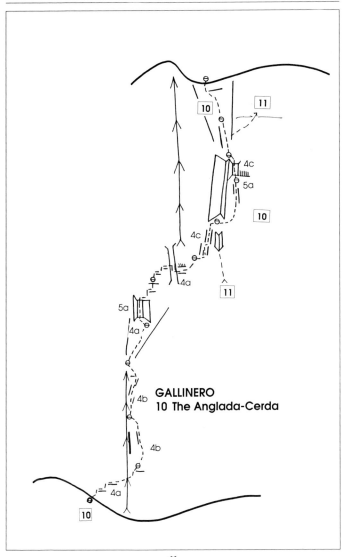

GALLINERO
10 The Anglada-Cerda

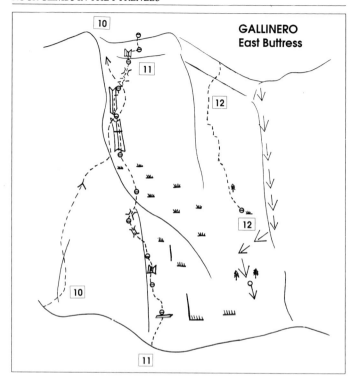

to a tree.

2) 25m. 4a. Climb ledges directly behind the tree to a smaller tree, traverse left delicately to a belay beneath a crack system.

3) 35m. 5b. Climb the fine jamming crack on the right to a break with a block ledge on the left. Continue up the bridging corner with difficulty to a belay on the left.

4) 25m. 5b. Return to the right and climb the slab and continuation crack to a belay on the left below a long dièdre.

5) 40m. 4c. Climb the dièdre to a belay on a chockstone.

6) 25m. 4a. Continue in the same line to a grassy terrace on the right.

7) 25m. 4a. The clean corner at the right end of the terrace leads to a tree and an exit.

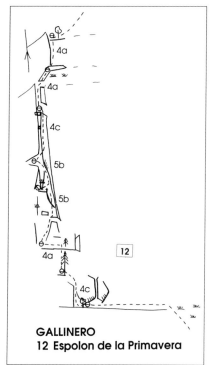

GALLINERO
12 Espolon de la Primavera

13. El Tridente, Diedro de los Vascos. MD. 150m. *
1st Ascent: 20th June 1971 - A.Alvira, J.L.Ariz, C.Santaquiteria and I.Tapia.

The route takes a couloir through the lower wall to gain the half-way terrace and then an obvious dièdre to the top where all the difficulties are met.

14. Los Cuervos. MD. 175m. *
1st Ascent: 11th July 1981 - Jesús Gálvez and Félix de Pablos.

Traverse in and climb the chimney. Good protection and a delight for practitioners of the technique.

15. Espolón Este, Rabadá-Navarro. ED. 390m. ***
1st Ascent: 15th-17th August 1961 - Alberto Rabadá and Ernesto Navarro.

A tremendous route and a much sought after prize. In typical Rabadá-Navarro style the line aims inexorably towards the immense overhangs below the hanging East Arête, avoids a loose band by an airy excursion to the right before climbing the crest of the buttress via a 120-metre dièdre. The crux pitch 150 metres above the path proves an irresistible attraction for any tourists in the area.

Start. At a regular dièdre capped by a triangular overhang 50m to the right of the line of the upper arête.

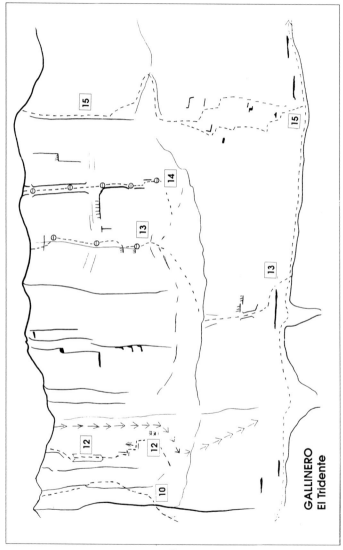

GALLINERO
El Tridente

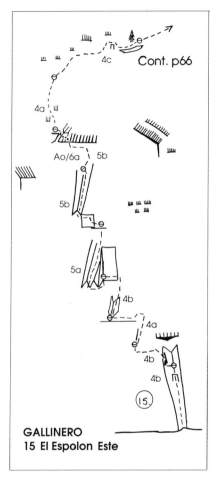

Cont. p66

GALLINERO
15 El Espolon Este

1) 40m. 4b. Climb the dièdre to a small platform.

2) 30m. 4b. Move left, climb a crack and go diagonally left to a wall and better rock.

3) 30m. 4a. Climb the wall for 15m and then traverse left along a good ledge.

4) 30m. 4b. Use small grooves to gain a good ledge in a smooth right-angled corner.

5) 30m. 5a. Go under the left-hand wall to the left-hand of two dièdres. Climb this, then cross to the right before coming back left to a good platform.

6) 30m. 5b. Cross the wall on the left in superb position and traverse to a fine crack which leads to a small belay under the huge roof.

7) 25m. 5b. Ao/6a. Gain the roof, cross the wall and move quickly into a niche in the lip. Bridge out of this to finish at a good platform on the left. An amazing pitch whether done free or Ao.

8) 20m. 4a. Up to a belay before the wall steepens.

9) 45m. 4c. Go diagonally right and then traverse right through a lunar landscape and poor rock to a ledge which leads easily to safe ground. Not a good place to fall off!

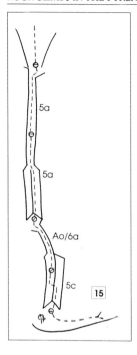

Skirt the subsidiary rocks of the upper half and come back left along an easy but very exposed ledge to the foot of a very steep grey dièdre which runs up to a left slanting chimney. There is a small bush at its foot and it is situated a few metres before an arête.

10) 25m. 5c. Climb the dièdre to a belay on the left.

11) 25m. Ao/6a. Continue up the chimney to a superb belay at the foot of the final dièdre.

12) 40m. 5a. 13) 40m. 5a. 14) -. Continue to the summit via the dièdre and chimney. A tired party may find these pitches a bit of an effort.

✳   ✳   ✳

LA FRAUCATA

This wall is less frequented than the others in the canyon and has a different 'feel.' The first route made on the wall, the Anglada-Cerdà-Eli, climbs a huge flying buttress inclined to the south, the only difficulties being met in the last 3 exit pitches which take a prominent dièdre. The second route done, La Via Barrabas, gives good value.

1. La Via Barrabas. MD. 325m.

1st Ascent: August 1977 - Serge Ballon and J.P.Barokas.

The route starts at a small tree 150m to the left of the Anglada and takes the line of least resistance up to the exit of that route.

RIGLOS

The climbing at Riglos is special for a number of reasons. The steepness and exposure, the improbability of lines up apparently blank walls, the spectacular descents and most of all the peculiar nature of the rock. The rock is described as conglomerate ('puddingstone') and comprises pebbles and medium sized rocks set into a hard sandstone, giving a profusion of holds with varying degrees of friction, usually good. Montserrat in the province of Cataluña and Meteora in Greece have similar areas. Although very steep or overhanging the walls are crossed by narrow, sloping ledges (cornisas) at intervals. Strength is an asset but a steady nerve pays handsome dividends when climbing here. It is possible to find nut runners but most of the routes are adequately equipped with bolts and pitons. Local climbers carry only extension slings and karabiners but first time visitors may find a small range of nuts gives a useful added security. The vast majority of the climbing is free but the occasional aid step does occur. Most of these steps go free and where known this is indicated in the description. Moves of 5b/5c or harder will (usually!) have a *situ* aid point at hand. The purist would be unwise to allow this to interfere with his enjoyment. Some routes have entire aid pitches and their positions usually reinforces the need for aid in certain circumstances, particularly when it allows a magnificent line to be completed.

Milestones in the history of climbing at Riglos are the first ascent of the Mallo Pison in 1946 by F.Peiré, J.Panyella and A.Murgia; 'El Puro' in 1953 by M.Bescós, A.Rabadá and A.López (said to have been climbed by los cojones!); the Rabadá-Navarro on the Firé in 1961 one of the greatest routes in Spain and 'La Carnavalada' by U.Abajo and J.Ibarzo in 1965, the first route to breach the imposing SW wall of the Mallo Pison. It is sometimes said that until one has done the Rabadá al Firé one hasn't climbed in Spain! The 1980's have seen a great interest in the number, quality and difficulty of routes opened, and the area is now one of major importance and interest.

It is possible to climb at Riglos all year round, but in mid-summer an early morning start is sensible to avoid the worst of the sun, while in winter it can be very cold and windy and some routes are rather long for short days.

No description of Riglos would be complete without mention of the vultures which inhabit the area, circling the towers or resting in

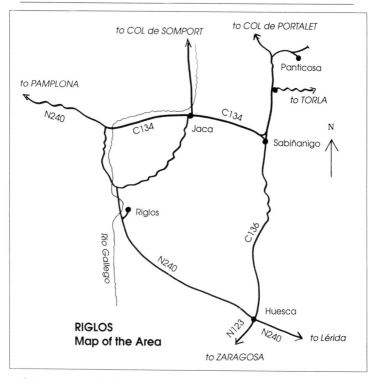

RIGLOS
Map of the Area

their eyries. To look up or even down onto these huge birds from a hanging stance and to wonder whether or not one is trespassing can be a thought-provoking experience.

The village of Riglos, which gives the crag its name, has a small hut, el refugio 'Gomez Laguna,' two bars and a swimming pool, but many climbers come either just for the day or bivvy at the end of the road which leads through the village and up to the foot of the Mallo Pison. All the routes are only a short walk from this road. Delicious fresh bread can be bought from the ancient bakery in the village of Murillo on the other side of the valley.

White water canoe enthusiasts will find the rio Gallego which flows through the valley from the 'embalse de la Peña' of great interest, amateurs even more so.

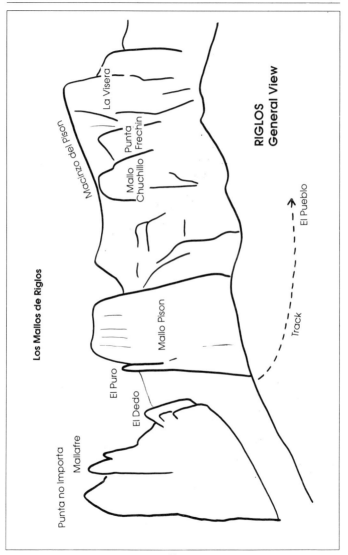

Los Mallos de Riglos

RIGLOS
General View

Macinzo del Pison

La Visera

Punta Frechin

Mallo Chuchillo

El Pueblo

Track

Mallo Pison

El Puro

El Dedo

Punta no Importa
Mallafre

Mallo Fire, Riglos Photo: A. Harmon

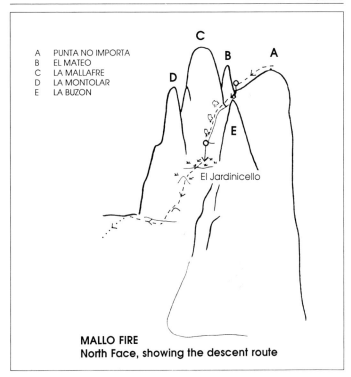

A   PUNTA NO IMPORTA
B   EL MATEO
C   LA MALLAFRE
D   LA MONTOLAR
E   LA BUZON

El Jardinicello

MALLO FIRE
North Face, showing the descent route

MALLO FIRE

Descent from the routes is shown in Diagram 31. It comprises two short abseils and some easy scrambling down the N flank in order to gain a broad col on the NE side of the Fire.

1. Galletas (Biscuits). MD. 300m. *
1st Ascent: 26th, 27th March 1959 - A.Rabadá and R.Montaner.

A friable old favourite giving a stern test of character.

Start. A large chimney-couloir separates the Punta No Importa and Mallafre. The route climbs this chimney and starts about 50m to its right at the foot of a mossy wall.

   1) 25m. 4b. Climb the wall diagonally leftwards to gain the

71

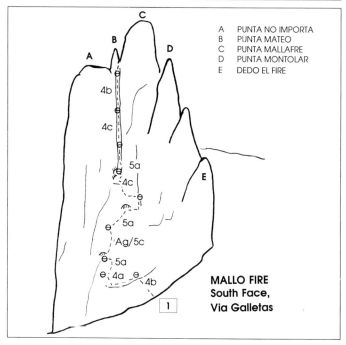

A PUNTA NO IMPORTA
B PUNTA MATEO
C PUNTA MALLAFRE
D PUNTA MONTOLAR
E DEDO EL FIRE

4b
4c
5a
4c
5a
Ag/5c
5a
4a   4b

MALLO FIRE
South Face,
Via Galletas

1

obvious traverse line.

2) 40m. 4a. Traverse left along the ledge to a broken corner and climb this to a good belay.

3) 25m. 4c. Climb the compact wall on the right of the belay until it is possible to move left to a good stance under an overhang.

4) 20m. 5c. Step right and move up to a very steep wall which is climbed to a good stance on the left under another overhang.

5) 40m. 5a. Climb diagonally right to a large niche containing a bush. Continue rightwards and then climb a short wall on suspect rock to a stance at the bottom of a long dièdre.

6) 45m. 4b. Traverse left and then climb a shallow corner to the huge chimney. Belay on the left above the first bulge.

7) 4c. 8) 4c. 9) 4b. Tremendous climbing for three pitches up the dièdre and then the chimney to the exit groove. Unusual situations.

Descent
Pick up the descent at the scramble down to the second abseil.

2.   The Rabadá-Navarro (SE Buttress).   MD+   385m.   *** ·
1st Ascent: 12th-16th October 1961 - Alberto Rabadá and Ernesto Navarro.

The two Aragonese climbers, who worked together in Zaragosa were responsible for many tremendous routes from the 1950's up to 1963, and none more so than this. It took six days of hard, free climbing and is a masterpiece of route finding, taking the line of least resistance up the crest of the buttress but without ignoring its challenge. Many variations exist but the route described is the best and differs from the original only on pitches 2 and 3. The dauntless pair did not use bolts on the first ascent, despite the availability, and a repetition of the route in its present bolt-protected state leaves one in no doubt that one has walked in the steps of the greats. Rabadá and Navarro died on the Eigerwand in August 1963 during a period of extremely bad storms; a grievous loss.

The route is a 'must' in any ambitious visitor's itinerary; once seen always contemplated; once climbed never forgotten.

Start.   15m to the right of the lowest point of the buttress.
1) 25m. 5c/Ao. Climb diagonally left to a niche at the foot of a short dièdre. Go up the dièdre until it is possible to traverse left to a good belay in large niche.
2) 35m. 4a. Climb the bulge on the right using two bolts and then traverse left, passing two dièdres to a belay on the other side of the buttress at the foot of a black, mossy wall which leans back a little. This belay is directly below the obvious West Couloir.
3) 40m. 4a. Climb the wall for 15m and then go diagonally left along a weakness until it is possible to go diagonally right to belay on a ledge, below an overhang, directly above the previous belay.
4) 35m. 5b. Descend to the right for 5m and traverse rightwards, going under several blocks until a thin crack is reached. Go up this and traverse around the corner on the right to belay in a small niche and on an even smaller ledge directly above the start of the route. Up to the right is a large red dièdre, the 'cicatriz.' A very exposed pitch.
5) 25m. 5a. Go diagonally leftwards over a variety of bulges to a good belay in the centre of the buttress.
6) 40m. 4c. Climb the wall behind the belay, zig-zagging around

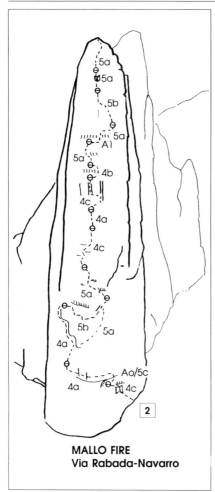

MALLO FIRE
Via Rabada-Navarro

bulges to belay on a good ledge where the wall starts to lean back.

7) 45m. 5a. Above are three chimneys. Climb up to and into the base of the rightmost chimney, traverse into the base of the centremost and climb it, passing a small tree to a belay.

8) 15m. 4a. Take the bulge above on the right and belay directly above the previous belay.

9) 30m. 5b. Climb the short groove behind the belay and make a rising traverse to the left across a compact wall to reach a loose groove. Climb this and then move right to belay on a ledge which runs all the way across the wall.

10) 25m. 5a. A1. (One step). Traverse 10m right and go over the bulge with the aid of a bolt (or use combined tactics as on the first ascent). Trend diagonally right and belay on the East Face of the final tower, directly opposite the Mallo Pison and in tremendous position.

11) 45m. 5b. 5c/Ao. Climb the compact wall behind the belay using the occasional aid point for 30m until it is possible to move left around the arête. Continue up to another small ledge.

12) 25m. 5a. Climb up to a short, shallow dièdre. Climb it using

a crack on the right to leave it before belaying on the left.

13) 40m. 5a. Climb directly, difficult at first and then with progressive ease to reach the summit of a truly memorable route.

Descent
Walk along the ridge to the short, diagonal abseil which starts the descent.

3. Traverse of the 5 peaks. D-
Only of interest to 'pinnacle baggers.'
From the foot of the Mallo Pison follow the path which leads to the easy col on the NE side of the Fire. Go around the right-hand side of the ridge and climb easy slabs to a garden (el Jardincillo) which leads to a bay at the foot of four peaks.

Climb to the col between the Buzon and the Mateo by taking first the wall on the right (4b) and then a tree-filled gully. The Buzon may now be topped. From the col traverse right across the base of the

MALLO FIRE
Traverse of the 5 Peaks

Mateo for a few metres (known as 'the move of the route') (4c), very airy and then climb diagonally right until one can walk to the top of the Punta No Importa.

Return along the ridge and climb the Mateo, 4c, poor rock. abseil in the direction of the Buzon back to the col. In order to top the Mallafre, climb to a small tree between the Mallafre and Mateo, ascend a little and then move left to a couloir which leads to the top, 4c.

Abseil into the col between the Mallafre

and the Montolar and climb the Montolar, poor rock, but easy. From here two abseils lead back to the Jardincillo.

✳   ✳   ✳

MALLO PISON

The descent is shown in Diagrams p80 and p82. It consists of two abseils to the col on the E side of the summit tower and then a scramble and abseil down a couloir 100m to the SE of the Pany-Haus chimney.

Descent from the Puro more or less follows the ordinary route and may be picked out during the ascent. The penultimate abseil is rightly famous.

4. Via de Verano. MD. 270m. *
1st Ascent: 18th September 1964 - U.Abajo and A.Peralta.

A magnificent route which avoids the initial overhangs via an excursion to the left and then follows a line of cracks to the summit. Retreat could be difficult.

5. Espolon Norte Integral (N.Buttress Direct). MD. 300m. *
1st Ascent: 19th, 20th May 1975 - A. del Corral, A.Garcia-Izquierdo, V.Asensio and F. Orús.

Start.   50m to the left of the lowest point of the buttress.
Should retreat be necessary, a bolt station at the 5th belay allows an abseil back to the Puro crack.

6. El Puro (The Cigar). Ordinary Route. MD- 260m. ***
1st Ascent: 13th, 14th, July 1953 - Manuel Bescos, Alberto Rabadá, Angel López, in competition with a party from Barcelona led by Panyella.

The first appearance of Rabadá on the climbing scene. The spire, historically famous, was given the name Franco after the Spanish head of state, but the climbing world has always called it el Puro.

The route spirals the Puro in clockwise fashion.

Start.   20m right of the point at which the car track meets the base of the wall, directly below the summit of the Puro.

   1) 30m. 4a. Climb diagonally left to a good ledge 5m below a

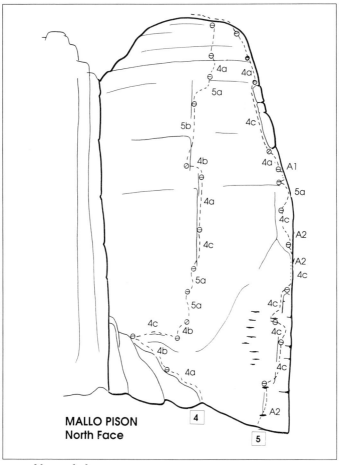

MALLO PISON
North Face

4

5

second larger ledge.

2) 30m. Traverse horizontally left for 13m and climb a short steep wall, 4c, to the next ledge. Follow this to the left to the base of a magnificent overhanging crack.

3) 30m. 5a. Climb the crack to a good ledge on the right.

4) 20m. 4a. Continue up the crack for 3m and then go diagonally

right to a belay just short of a cave guarding the entrance to the Puro chimney.

5) 25m. 5b. Climb the cave roof by its left side and continue up the couloir to a belay on the right.

6) 35m. 7) 15m. 4a. Pleasant climbing up the chimney to a belay under a block jammed between the Puro and the main wall. The south face of the upper section of the Puro may now be seen.

8) 20m. 4c. Start up the right arête and trend leftwards, passing a prominent oblong block to a good ledge below a small overhang.

9) 45m. 5b. Climb the overhang directly above the belay and go up to a second ledge. Leave this slightly on the right and reach a third ledge. Leave this, again slightly on the right (Ao/6a) and continue to the summit passing yet another ledge. It is probably better to gain the summit by spiralling right from the last ledge.

El Puro the final pitch, Riglos
Climbers: D.L. Walker
D.W. Walsh T. Hughes
Photo: P. Miller

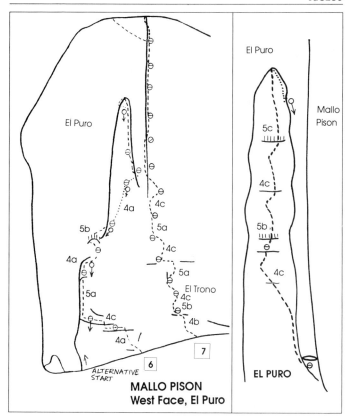

MALLO PISON
West Face, El Puro

EL PURO

Descent

From the summit a cable leads to the north and then round to the east to where the normal abseil descent starts, about 10m below the summit.

NB. A direct start may be made up the chimney crack which leads to the second belay. A well-protected (nuts) 4c bridging pitch.

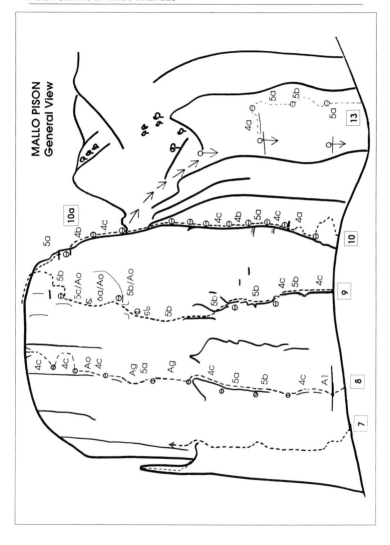

MALLO PISON
General View

7. Serón-Millan. MD. 300m.
1st Ascent: 20th-22nd July 1957 - A.Rabadá, A.López, J.J.Diaz and R.Montaner. (The route was dedicated to the first climbers at Riglos.)

This route follows an obvious break running up to the couloir which starts from the base of the Puro. It is a little loose, wanders somewhat and hence has been neglected in favour of the routes to its right. The couloir, however, is done in combination with the Puro. Its grade is VS and is usually completed by traversing left after the last belay.

8. La Carnavalada. MD- 270m. **
1st Ascent: 9th-13th October 1965 - Ursi Abaja and Jesus Ibarzo.

A very direct line, much sought after in the 60's, with no route finding problems.

Start at the 'Cueva de la Virgen' (cave) and climb to the top.

9. Via Alberto Rabadá. MD. 270m. ***
1st Ascent: January 1976 - Miguel and Angel Gallego.

The leader dedicated the route to the great Spanish climber, however, as the brothers came from the province of Murcia it is also known as the 'Murciana.'
    A super route, free at 5b apart from the aid bulges on the last three pitches, though these go at a strenuous 6a. Well-protected.

Start.   At a large flake corner about 25m left of the Pany-Haus chimney.
    1) 45m. 5b. The corner crack to the top of a pedestal.
    2) 30m. 5a. Continue to a hanging stance.
    3) 45m. 5b. Up and then diagonally left and then up again to another hanging stance.
    4, 5) 70m. 5b. Continue in the same line to belay on a ledge 'big enough for two people!'
    6) 20m. 5b. Diagonally left and then over the bulge, Ao.
    7) 30m. 5b. Slightly right and over another bulge.
    8) 30m. 5b. Right again and over the last bulge to finish easily.

10. Vìa Pany-Haus. D. ***
1st Ascent: 28th June 1948 - Jorge Panyella and Alberto Casasallas (nickname Haus).

The most popular route on the massif, leading to the col at the base of the final tower in 240m.

1, 2) Climbed with short excursions to the right

3) 5a. Bridge the overhang for a taste of what is to come.

4) 5c. For those with short legs climb the right wall quickly or Ao.

5, 6, 7) Good and interesting climbing to easy ground.

The Pany may be combined with the Normal on the Torreon del Pison, also D, which leads to the summit in a further 3 pitches on excellent rock in good position and with views of the village roofs.

1) 30m. 4c. A rising traverse to the left followed by easy climbing to a belay slightly on the left.

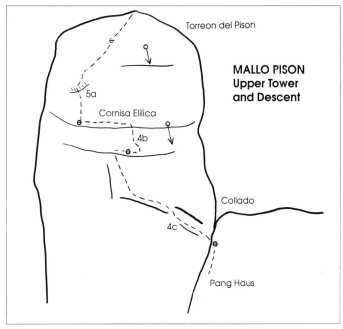

2) 30m. 4b. Climb the arête on the right of the belay to a ledge then traverse 15m left to the belay.

3) 40m. 5a. Climb the bulge up to the left then go easily rightwards to the summit of the Pison.

11. Via Adamelo. MD- (HVS. 5b.) 170m.
1st Ascent: 22nd August 1965 - U.Abajo and J.Ibarzo.

A nice route, though short, which climbs the prominent arête to the right of the Pany-Haus chimney.

Start. At the foot of the arête.

1) 40m. 4c. Climb slightly on the left of the arête for 20m and then go over bulges directly on the arête to belay on a good ledge.

2) 15m. 5b. Go over the overhang on the right of the belay and then directly up to another ledge.

3) 30m. 4b. Traverse right and then up and back to the arête to a further ledge below a small overhang.

4) 20m. 4c. Move left, go over the overhang and climb directly to a good belay.

5) 40m. 4a. Climb easily up poor rock to a belay on the right of the couloir.

6) 25m. 4a. Continue easily to the top passing a tree and finally traversing right.

Descent
Traverse right until one can join the normal descent from the Mallo Pison. It is possible, and may be preferable, to descend the line of the route by abseil after pitch 4, assuming no other parties are below.

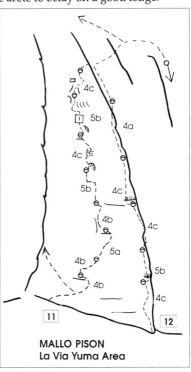

MALLO PISON
La Via Yuma Area

12.   Via Yuma.   MD.   180m.
1st Ascent: 27th August 1981 - E.Lapeña and M.A.Lausin.

A meandering route, hard and on good rock, popular. The last two pitches are often omitted and a traverse made to Adamelo which is then descended by abseil.

13.   Via Anis del Mono.   MD-   150m.
1st Ascent: 3rd October 1982 - E.Lapeña, A.Oliver and O.Olivar.

Short but good.
Start.   A few metres to the left of the arête.
    1, 2, 3) Climb directly to the Cornisa de les Volados.
    4) Move left and down for a few metres and then traverse easily to the abseil point of the normal descent.

✳   ✳   ✳

LA VISERA
Descent
This is easy, along the ridge to the east before descending a path 150m beyond the via Torrijo.
    The face is well seen from the road approaching the village. The rock is good and the steepness awe inspiring. Some routes here overhang for a full 300m but go completely free.

14.   Via Guirles-Campos.   MD   270m.   *
1st Ascent: July 1978 - D.Guirles and L.Campos.

The right-hand side of the Visera is a leaning wall which overhangs more and more the higher it becomes. The first part of the route follows the blunt arête which forms the left edge of the wall whilst the second part follows an open grey couloir in the face to the left.

Start.   At a small buttress with a chimney on its right.
    1) Climb the chimney to a platform.
    2, 3, 4) 80m. 5a. Follow the arête to a belay on the left.
    5,6,7,8,9) 120m. 5b, 5a. Climb diagonally left for a pitch and then directly to the foot of the grey couloir.
    10, 11, 12) Follow the couloir diagonally right to the summit.

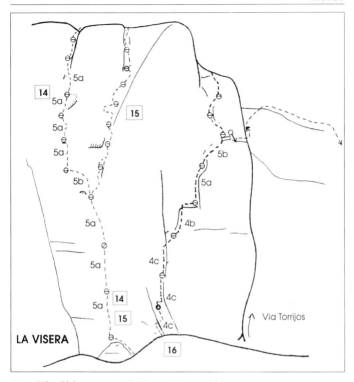

LA VISERA

Via Torrijos

15. Via Chinatown. MD+ 270m. ***
1st Ascent: September 1983 - F.Caballé, F.Gutierrez, S.Buennaudas, 'Shaino.'

A hard, strenuous and superb route.
Follow the Guirles-Campos for 4 pitches and then follow the edge of the overhanging face for a further 6 pitches. Use a vague grey couloir for 2 more pitches to gain the summit.

16. Via Mosquitos. MD- 270m. **
1st Ascent: 27th June 1976 - J.Olivar and A.Sanchez.

A good route now totally free. Many parties escape from 'El Trono' (the Throne) by making a 7m abseil to a ledge leading off right rather than doing the last three pitches up to 'El Hombro' (the Shoulder) which are harder and more strenuous than those preceding.

Start.   At the highest point of the approach slope is a faint dièdre. 5m left is another more prominent dièdre slanting leftwards. The climb starts in this one.

1) 20m. 4c. Climb the dièdre for 10m, traverse right for a few metres and then go over two bulges to a good ledge.

2) 25m. 4c. Go over the bulge just right of the belay, move right into the prominent crack and climb it to a stance at the foot of a fine corner.

3) 35m. 4c. Climb the corner for 30m and then traverse the right-hand wall to a ledge near the arête.

4) 20m. 4b. Climb the broken groove avoiding some loose rock to a large platform.

5) 35m. 4c. From the right-hand end of the platform climb the superb crack to a belay where the angle eases.

6) 35m. 5a. Climb diagonally right, first up cracks and then traverse a wall in good position (a fall here would be interesting) until one can make a dignified move on to 'El Trono,' an enormous block perched on the wall.

7, 8) 50m. 5b. Climb diagonally left to gain the foot of a couloir, climb it and then traverse right to belay on a large platform.

9) 50m. Climb directly, difficult for a few metres, until easier climbing leads to the top.

THE VIGNEMALE   3,298m

The Vignemale is a high, remote, limestone massif situated on the French-Spanish border midway between Cauterets and Torla. Possessing several glaciers it is an excellent area for both mountaineering and rock climbing. The North Face is particularly impressive and is where the majority of the harder rock routes are to be found. A hanging valley, the Oulettes de Gaube, is the normal pre-route staging point where is also to be found a hut.

The easiest approach is from the north by car through Cauterets to Pont d'Espagne and then a 3-hour walk along the beautiful Vallée de Gaube. From Spain it may be approached on foot by using the Rio Ara and then the Col des Mulets. The Rio Ara leads directly from Torla, but it may also be gained from Balneario de Panticosa via the Ibones de Bramatuero and the Collado de Letrero.

Descents
Petit Vignemale
Easily to the north-east slightly on the right of the arête to the Hourquette d'Ossoue, the col between the refuge Baysellance, and then the path to the Oulettes de Gaube.

Pointe de Chausenque, Piton Carre, Pique Longue
Easy rock to the north drops to the Grand Glacier d'Ossoue. This leads to the east, eventually skirting the E arête of the Petit Vignemale before giving access to the refuge Baysellance.

GRAND VIGNEMALE   (3,298m)
Pique-Longue
This is the highest summit on the massif. Many routes to this peak exist, most of them being best done in winter or spring. (See also R9, R10.)

1.   Ordinary route via the Glacier d'Ossoue.   F.
From the Oulettes de Gaube take the path du Centenaire across the plateau to the south which eventually climbs east to the Col la Hourquette d'Ossoue and then descends to the refuge Baysellance (2 hours). From here follow the path to Gavarnie around the ENE arête of the Petit Vignemale and then leave it by crossing horizontally to

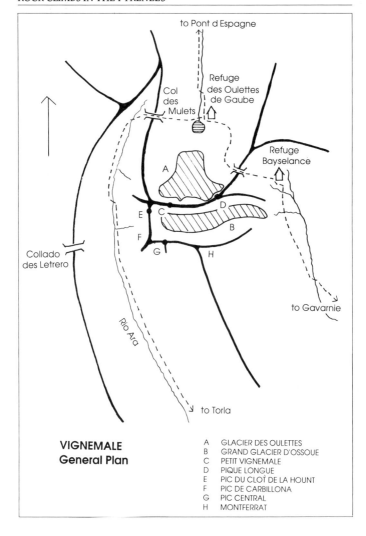

to Pont d Espagne

Col
des
Mulets

Refuge
des Oulettes
de Gaube

Refuge
Bayselance

A

C D

E
F

G H

Collado
des Letrero

B

Rio Ara

to Gavarnie

to Torla

VIGNEMALE
General Plan

A	GLACIER DES OULETTES
B	GRAND GLACIER D'OSSOUE
C	PETIT VIGNEMALE
D	PIQUE LONGUE
E	PIC DU CLOT DE LA HOUNT
F	PIC DE CARBILLONA
G	PIC CENTRAL
H	MONTFERRAT

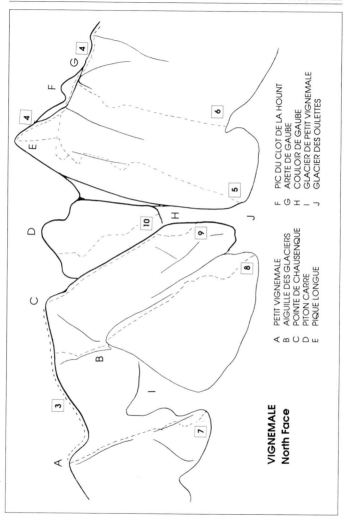

VIGNEMALE
North Face

A PETIT VIGNEMALE
B AIGUILLE DES GLACIERS
C POINTE DE CHAUSENQUE
D PITON CARRE
E PIQUE LONGUE

F PIC DU CLOT DE LA HOUNT
G ARETE DE GAUBE
H COULOIR DE GAUBE
I GLACIER DE PETIT VIGNEMALE
J GLACIER DES OULETTES

89

the west to gain the Glacier d'Ossoue. Take the easiest line to the plateau below the summit cone. The summit may be gained up easy-angled rocks. ($4^{1}/2$ hours).

This is the usual descent for routes on the N side of the mountain.

2.   L'Arête du Montferrat.   PD-

If the central section of the Glacier d'Ossoue is undesirable, it may be avoided by traversing left under its eastern extremity and then climbing the arête which bounds it on the south. The arête is left before the summit of Montferrat in order to reach the glacier plateau as before, which is usually crevassed also.

3.   L'Arête Petit Vignemale (3,032m) - Pointe de Chausenque (3,205m).   AD-

This is a popular outing. From the Col la Hourquette follow the ridge to the summit of the Petit Vignemale and then continue, with a little difficulty in the first 100m, passing the Col des Glaciers and a shoulder at 3,138m to reach the Pointe de Chausenque. From here descend to the upper part of the Glacier d'Ossoue.

4.   L'Arête de Gaube.   AD+

This is the western arête which overlooks the north face and the Glacier des Oulettes.

From the Glacier des Oulettes a small amphitheatre containing snow is seen high on the north flank of the arête. Gain this by climbing a rib of green ophite rock for 100m and then continuing diagonally right. Leave the amphitheatre by going first right and then left and so reach the Arête de Gaube. Continue up the arête to reach the summit cone.

Climb steeply for 10 metres, move right for a few metres and climb a block, above which come back left to a steep wall. Avoid this by going diagonally right to a dièdre, which is climbed for a few metres until it is possible to climb an easy chimney on the left. By climbing slightly on the right some walls lead to a brèche on the other side of which easy slopes lead to the summit. ($4^{1}/2$ hours)

The Arête de Gaube may be gained easily from the Rio Ara by following the Rio Viñamale and then the north side of the Glacier du Clot de la Hount.

✳   ✳   ✳

PIQUE LONGUE
5. North Face by the Classic Route.   D+   850m.   ***
1st Ascent: 8th August 1933 - H.Barrio and Bellocq.

One of the most famous and longest outings in the area. A magnificent route in magnificent surroundings, sustained but without great technical difficulty.

The route follows the 'Intermediate Arête' to its top, traverses left along the 'schistes-rouge' and then offers two finishes. Many variations are possible but the way described is generally considered to be the classic.

Start.   From the Oulettes de Gaube, climb the Glacier des Oulettes to a point about 30m below the bergschrund of the Couloir de Gaube, just to the right of the rib seen high on the face. The wall is marked by a thin green ophite rib.

Climb the wall for a few metres, traverse right to a vague chimney and go up to a good terrace, 4a.

Move left towards the Couloir de Gaube and climb the buttress for 4 or 5 pitches, first towards the Intermediate Arête and then as difficulties are met, slightly right across open slabs towards the Cheminee des Autrichiens. Upon reaching the level of the base of the Intermediate Arête, use a pleasant dièdre to go around to its left-hand side and gain an enormous amphitheatre overlooking the Pointe de Chausenque.

On the left a thin rib of green ophite rock will be seen running up to the arête on the right. Climb this and then the arête, in three delightful pitches to a gendarme and small brèche. Descend to the left a little and then climb a crack back to the arête and another brèche, dominated by a very steep buttress, 4a. Steps of 4b.

Go round to the right of the buttress and use a flake to gain a small platform in the centre of the buttress just above one crack and below a second steep crack which runs up the crest. Climb this, 4c, and then continue by the line of least resistance for three pitches to where the arête ends and the level of the schistes-rouge is reached.

A long, delicate traverse left, best taken at a high level, leads to a blunt arête which is followed for two further pitches to an airy belay in the wall above the termination of this other arête, 4b.

From here two finishes are possible:-
1) Climb diagonally left to the obvious couloir running down from the summit. Four pitches, harder and more strenuous than anything

else on the route, or

2) More usual, climb diagonally right to the Arête de Gaube in one pitch and finish via this route. Three pitches; climb directly for 10 metres and then zig-zag by the line of least resistance, using an easy chimney.

6.   North Buttress.   ED.   500m.
1st Ascent: 19th, 20th July 1964 - Bernard Grenier, J.Ravier and P.Ravier

The major difficulties lie in the final 100m. The rock is not too good and a lot of aid is used.

*   *   *

PETIT VIGNEMALE
7.   The N.W. Buttress.   D.   400m.   *
1st Ascent: 6th August 1947 - R.Cazanave and C.Subot.

A pleasant route.

Start.   At the toe of the buttress where a ramp slants from right to left.

1) 30m.   Ascend the ramp to belay at the foot of a V-shaped weakness.

2) 30m. 4c. Climb the open dièdre exiting left to a good terrace.

3) 40m. 4a. Continue up the rib on the left to where the angle eases.

4) 4a. 5) 4a. Go diagonally right across open slabs to belay in a col behind a very prominent gendarme. A variety of paths are available.

6) 4a. 7) 4a. Move right to the wall overlooking the Glacier du Petit Vignemale and gain a chimney groove. Follow this to the arête.

Easy climbing leads to the summit wall, where couloirs eventually give access to the summit.

*   *   *

AIGUILLE DES GLACIERS
8.   N.W. Buttress.   D.   500m.
1st Ascent: 23rd August 1946 - G.Chabanneau and R.Ollivier.

The route follows the arête more or less directly, with only two difficult sections.
   The opening wall may be taken slightly on the right (west) or by a detour to the left; easier but on poorer rock. At mid-height a line of overhangs is met which are turned on the right. From the summit a ledge system leads leftwards (SE) above the Glacier du Petit Vignemale to the col on the main ridge which runs from the Petit-Vignemale to the Pointe de Chausenque.

✳   ✳   ✳

PITON CARRE OU JUMEAUX   (3,198m)
9.   North Face.   TD.   400m.   *
1st Ascent: 31st July 1954 - Jacques Teillard, J.Ravier and P.Ravier.

Although only graded TD, this route can be found to be very difficult indeed because of verglas and is in reality a mixed route.

✳   ✳   ✳

POINTE DE CHAUSENQUE   (3,205m)
10.   N.W. Buttress.   TD.   700m.   **
1st Ascent: 4th July 1945 - F.Boyrie and J.Simpson.

A big route.

Start.   Ascend the glacier and cross the bergschrund of the Couloir de Gaube. Continue a further 80m to a point about 20m past a diagonal weakness which is the prominent feature of the lower part of the buttress.
   Go left to a steep wall and the major difficulties. Either make a detour to the left or, more easily, climb a leaning crack to gain a chimney which gives access to the crest of the buttress. Follow the crest to the summit with short excursions to the right to avoid difficulties.

✳   ✳   ✳

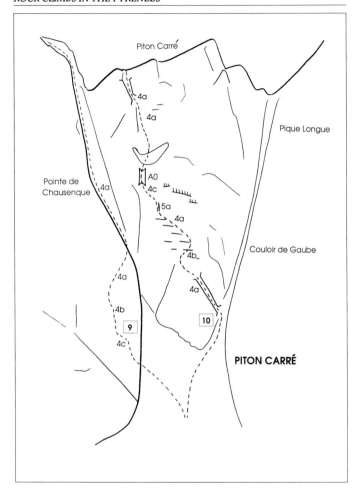

Piton Carré

Pique Longue

Pointe de
Chausenque

Couloir de Gaube

PITON CARRÉ

94

LA VALLÉ DE TENA

This large and beautiful valley extends southwards from the Col de Portalet and the Midi d'Ossau, following the Rio Gallego to Biescas from where the road to Torla and Ordesa commences. It includes many peaks, lakes and villages, much rock and the important side valley containing Panticosa; a gateway by foot to the Vignemale, Gavarnie and Ordesa. In summer a multitude of walks, scrambles and easy peak bagging can be done as well as wind surfing, paragliding and other typical summer sports. In winter, snow-ice routes can be added to the itinerary besides skiing in the resorts of Panticosa and Formigal whose lifts give quick and effortless access to many of the peaks. The rapidly developing escuela of 'Las Foronias' is situated alongside the road from Panticosa to the spa of Balneario, where it is possible to climb all year round. The villages have an archetypal Spanish Pyrenees atmosphere where the people are open, warm and generous. Climbers are welcome in the bars and restaurants, which are many and whose prices are inexpensive. The natural climbing centre for the area is Panticosa.

In an area with as much rock as the Vallé de Tena the new route list features many names, but one man stands out. Ursi Abajo climbed many magnificent lines throughout the valley in the 60's and 70's and none more grand than the Gran Diedro on the Peña Telera.

LA SIERRA DE PARTACUA (TELERA)

Known by climbers as the Peña Telera, this chain, over 10 km long, bounds and dominates the valley on its south-west and gives a more or less continuous wall of 600m interrupted by peaks and gullies. The limestone is generally regarded as poor though well over 50 long routes have been done, some of which have improved dramatically over the years. In the cold months however the sierra gives many very fine snow-ice routes and is a major area for winter exploration. The routes selected here are on the Peña Telera itself, the most impressive peak and wall in the chain. The peak is approached by leaving the main road N134bis at Lake Bubal and following the road to Piedrafita. Continue a further 3 km past the village to a convenient point close to the small Ibón de Piedrafita.

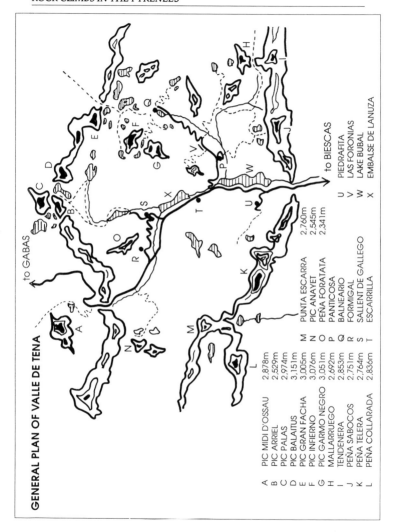

GENERAL PLAN OF VALLE DE TENA

to GABAS

to BIESCAS

A	PIC MIDI D'OSSAU	2,878m
B	PIC ARRIEL	2,529m
C	PIC PALAS	2,974m
D	PIC BALAITUS	3,151m
E	PIC GRAN FACHA	3,005m
F	PIC INFIERNO	3,076m
G	PIC GARMO NEGRO	3,051m
H	MALLARRUEGO	2,692m
I	TENDEÑERA	2,853m
J	PEÑA SABOCOS	2,751m
K	PEÑA TELERA	2,764m
L	PEÑA COLLARADA	2,836m
M	PUNTA ESCARRA	2,760m
N	PIC ANAYET	2,545m
O	PEÑA FORATATA	2,341m
P	PANTICOSA	
Q	BALNEARIO	
R	FORMIGAL	
S	SALLENT DE GALLEGO	
T	ESCARRILLA	
U	PIEDRAFITA	
V	LAS FORONIAS	
W	LAKE BUBAL	
X	EMBALSE DE LANUZA	

96

LA PENA TELERA   (2,764m)
Descent
Via the normal route.

1.   The Normal Route.   F.   1,300m.

Skirt the lake and gain the very typical col between the Corona del Mallo and the Cavichirizas via a scree-filled gully. Make a very airy and occasionally precarious traverse across the front of the Cavichirizas and then continue easily to the summit by a path up the SW slopes of the Peña Telera itself.

2.   Corredor Watadé.   250m.
1st Ascent: 19th September 1976 - J.Calvo, J.Berberana, J.M.Cebolleda, A.Chavarri and J.L.Lalaguna.
1st Winter: 30th January 1983 - J.López, J.P.Alvarez, G.Hernaez and A.Medinabeita.

This route is MD in summer but is more usually done as an excellent winter route, though it can be done under snow-ice conditions as late as June.

3.   Gran Diagonal.   AD.   1,000m.
1st Ascent: 12th August 1965 - J.R.Morandeira and L.Gutiérrez.
1st Winter: 18th March 1966 - Same team.

A more interesting outing than the normal route and again, an excellent winter route.

4.   Gran Diedro Norte.   ED-   700m.   ***
1st Ascent: 27th, 28th August 1970 - U.Abajo and Pierre Forn.
1st Winter: 22nd, 23rd January 1983 - A.Miranda, J.Ayarzábal, J.Luis and V.Perales.

A true 'North Wall,' so be prepared. The line is obvious.

❊   ❊   ❊

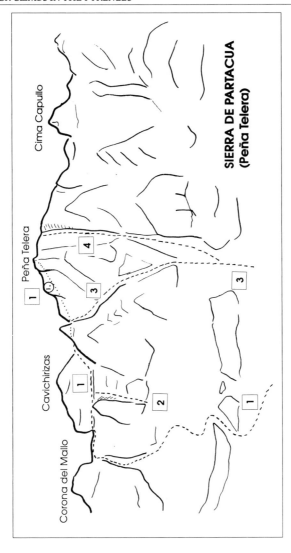

SIERRA DE PARTACUA
(Peña Telera)

EL PICO DE ANAYET   (2,545m)

This attractive peak is easily approached from the new road which leaves the main high-way halfway between Formigal and the Col de Portalet. Ten routes or variations have been done, four of which are described - all around 300m.

Descent
Via the ordinary route.

5.   Ordinary Route via the S.E. Face.   F.

This is the normal descent route and follows a path which crosses an exposed slab at one point but does not give any difficulty.

6.   The East Face.   D+   *
1st Ascent: 19th July 1975 - U.Abajo and P.Forn.

A good route which follows the obvious chimney crack cutting the face diagonally before finishing up a rib.

7.   The East Gully.   AD.
1st Ascent: 1925 - J.Arlaud, H.Marceillac and L.Mobbe.

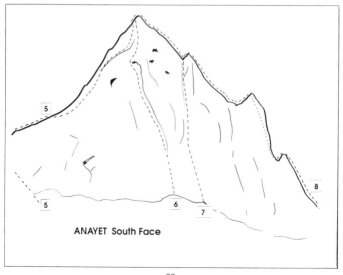

ANAYET South Face

The route follows the gully to the col and then the arête to the summit. Best done in winter when it gives an excellent snow-ice route.

8.   The North East Arête.   D.
1st Ascent: 7th April 1957 - J.J.Diaz and J.Vicente.

A nice ridge route with all the difficulties concentrated in the first two gendarmes. The second is climbed via its North Face.

✳   ✳   ✳

PENA FORATATA   (2,341m)
This very rocky peak is easily approached from the ski village of Formigal. A dozen routes up the obvious features have been done but the intervening walls are mostly untouched.

Descent
Via the ordinary route, of which there are two! The second may have the occasional loose rock fall.

9.   The Ordinary Route, North.   PD.   400m.
From Formigal walk up the pastures, heading left (west) in order to skirt the west ridge. Now traverse the North Face and approach the summit cone. Climb this via a chimney crack on the right which leads to the ridge and then the top.

10.   The Ordinary Route, South.   PD+   400m.
A large grass projection allows a gully to the right to be gained. This leads to a ledge which cuts across the South Face.

11.   The South West Couloir.   MD-   500m.   *
1st Ascent: 1968 - G.Villarig and J.López Vera.

The route starts by a large detached block. A chimney crack leads up over ledges, to the left, and then to a wide chimney. This is climbed to an exit right over vertical walls and then a twisting crack which is passed on the right via a small overhang and blocks. Difficult climbing up a smooth wall leads to a new crack and chimney which then gives on to a couloir on the left and the end of the difficulties.

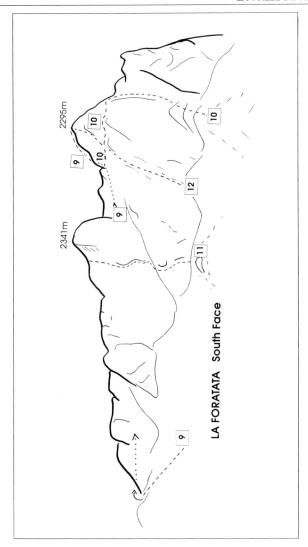

LA FORATATA South Face

12.   Via Villarig-Barcos. (S.W. Face).   D+   400m.
1st Ascent: G.Villarig and José Mª Barcos.

A nice route which is steady apart from the first and last pitches which are a little harder. It follows a couloir line.

✳   ✳   ✳

LA ESCUELA DE SANTA ELENA
This recently established escuela is situated on the north side of the valley which runs east from the N134bis 5 km north of Biescas, along the southern flank of the Peña de Hoz.

It is a roadside crag, the road being a car-worthy forest track which is passable for about 4 km, at the end of which will be found a hut and the excellent wall containing Gruyêre. Friction moves abound, descent is by abseil, most routes have good natural protection and several are destined to become classics when the valley is further developed. The crag is named after the ancient hermitage which overlooks the main road. The 'ermita' is flanked by old military fortifications and the wall to the right of the 'Triangulo,' a disused quarry, has derelict workings at its foot which give a useful marker. The picnic area beside the track comes complete with Stone Age dolmen. Routes Nos. 1-10 vary from 40m to 100m in length.

Pared del Puente
1.   Las Ardillas Tambien se Enamoran.   E2.   50m.
(F.Baratech, A.Esarpa, J.Larre and J.Oliver.)

El Triangulo
2.   Three Easy Lines.

Pared de la Cantera
3.   Eva Mescalito.   HVS.
(F.Baratech and J.Oliver.)

4.   Materia Descompuesta.   VS.
(E.Chillardu, J.Bazan, J.Oliver, F.Baratech and A.Escarpa.)

5.   Via de los Techos.   HVS.   A1.
(J.Oliver, F.Baratech and A.Escarpa.)

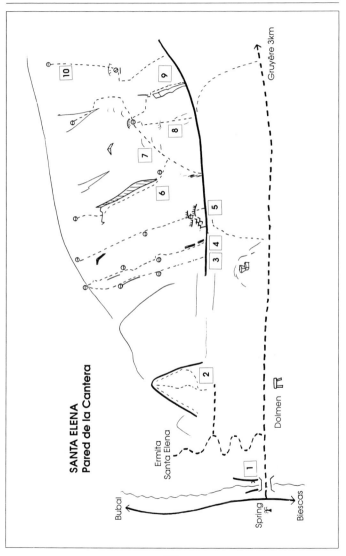

SANTA ELENA
Pared de la Cantera

Looking down pitch 2 of Gruyêre, Santa Elena
Climber: D. Reade Photo: A. Harman

6.   Elena y Tarzan en la Jungla Vertical.   VS.
(F.Baratech and A.Escarpa.)

7.   Via de los Tarras.   V.Diff.

8.   La Abuela Roquera. Direct.   HVS.   *
(D.L.Walker and D.Gale.)

The opening pitch of El Puro, Riglos, the Firé in the background.
Climber: D.L. Walker Photo: A. Harman

9. La Abuela Roquera. VS.
(A.Escarpa and F.Baratech.)

10. Anonymous. E2. **

11. Gruyêre. E2. 120m. ***
First Ascent: Ursi Abajo and son.

An excellent route.
From the hut continue up the track for 100m and then follow a path
to the wall.

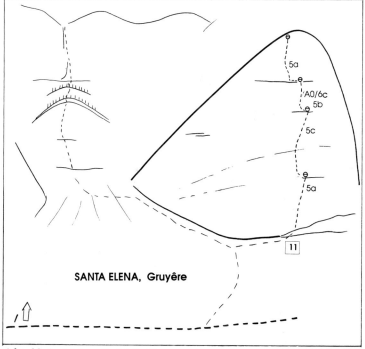

SANTA ELENA, Gruyêre

A hard bulge high on the Mallo Pison, Riglos.
Climber: unknown Photo: D.L. Walker

Start.   About 10m to the right of the lowest point of the wall.
1) 30m. 5a. Climb the broken wall and then the discontinuous crack line to a narrow ledge.
2) 35. 5c. Step left, and then climb directly to a horizontal break. Continue exquisitely up a weakness in the friction slab to a good ledge.
3) 15m. The wall above has nine bolts. Climb as far as possible free, 5c to the 7th and continue at Ao or 6b. A good test piece.
4) 40m. 5a. Move 5m left and then climb steeply to the top.

Descent
Abseil back down the route.

12.   A mixed route over the stepped overhangs done by U.Abajo. The final free pitch is very fine and is E2 6a.

13.   La Via Vicente.   E1.   140m.   *
First Ascent: 1989 - U.Abajo.

This route takes a very obvious dièdre in the cliff which runs along the west side of Lake Bubal, very obvious from the road on the other side of the lake. From the main road running south to Biescas, take the small road to Hoz which crosses the dam and leave the car at a convenient point in order to descend to the lake. Follow the lakeside north until the trees thin and then scramble up right to the dièdre.

   The dièdre gives four good pitches, 5a/b, well protected by bolts, in good position. The rock is rather dirty and a little loose in one section, but should improve with use to give a good route.

   In 1989 two other good routes were added to the Gruyère wall by Ursi Abajo. The walls between the Pared de la Cantera and Gruyère are very extensive. A route was done in 1988 by A.Harmon and I.R.Jones, **Derek's Dilemma, 120m. E1. 5a,** situated approximately half-way up the valley and marked by situ slings.

＊   ＊   ＊

LAS FORONIAS

The escuela of las Foronias is situated on the north side of the road leading from Panticosa to Balneario next to the stream of the same name. 1 km from the village, and only 10m from the road and facing south the crag is ideal should the weather be adverse in the mountains. It makes a fine play area in the evenings or for a quiet day if staying in Panticosa. Climbing is possible all year round and it is not unusual to be in shirt sleeves at Christmas while surrounded by snow-capped peaks and ski aficionados.

Made of limestone having excellent friction, it dries in hours and gives varied climbing as the type of hold differs from wall to wall. Although 150m high, the development is for single pitch or 50m routes and despite adequate natural protection, bolts are appearing on some lines as is the case in many areas of Europe. However, local climbers have a lengthy discussion before drilling, and so far have preferred new routes to be done from the bottom (*desde abajo*) other than for gardening. Care is needed in some places as the crag is still young but the potential of the area is unlimited, especially if one is prepared to move away from the roadside to the other, as yet untouched, areas.

The cliff was opened up through the efforts of Julio Armesta, Enrique Villasur and Fernando Guzman in 1984 with the Zodiac Routes. Derek Walker along with Stuart Smith climbed La Mano Blanca' (The White Hand) in 1985 after spotting the route on a ski trip and then started to tap the tremendous potential of the Black Wall area. This 75° wall gives immaculate slab-type climbing on a myriad of very small holds. Easter 1986 saw the first open route on the wall, 'La Mano Negra' (The Black Hand - named after a cartoon character in the Spanish climbing magazine *Alto Ruta*) by Walker and Dave Walsh and also the first pitch of 'Oxession Consumada,' on sight, by the same pair after an initial attempt by Smith. Unfortunately the route was bolted from above by a team from Zaragosa though it still saw several notable failures before Armesta made the second ascent.

A new route book is kept in the bar Navarro which is in the centre of Panticosa, where also will be found Julio Armesta who will give advice on this and other crags in the area.

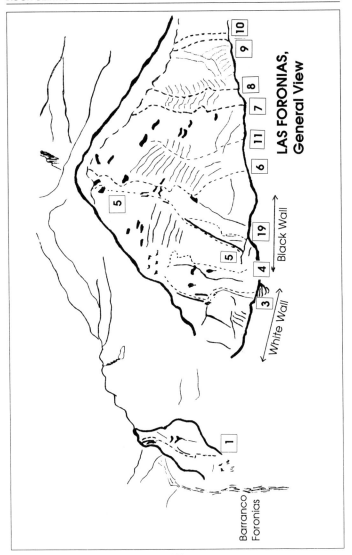

LAS FORONIAS, General View

Black Wall

White Wall

Barranco Foronias

Zodiac Routes
1. Cancer. E2. 5b, 5c, 5a. 60m. *
Airy.

2. Aries. E4. 5a, 6b, 4a. 60m. **
Strenuous.

3. Geminis. VS. 4c, 4c. 100m. *
The first route on the crag.

4. Leo. HVS. - - 5b, 4c. 80m.

5. Capricornio. HVS. 4b, 4c, 4c, 5a. 150m. ***
An enjoyable route.

6. Escorpio. E1. 5a, 5b, 5b, 4a. 140m. *

7. Libra. E1. 5b, 4b, 5a. 100m.
A strenuous first pitch.

8. Piscis. HVS. 5b, 4b. 65m.
A natural line.

9. Tauro. VS. 5a, 4b. 50m.
Pleasant.

10. Acuario. VS. 5a. 50m.
Similar to Tauro.

11. Virgo.
Incomplete, a very impressive line!

Other routes:-

12. El Dedo Muerto (Dead Finger Crack). E1. 5c. 30m. *
1st Ascent: 23rd April 1987 - C.Nunn and D.Gale.

A good direct line.

13. Vanilla. VS. 4c. 45m.
1st Ascent: 13th April 1987 - I.R.Jones, D.L.Walker and D.Gale.

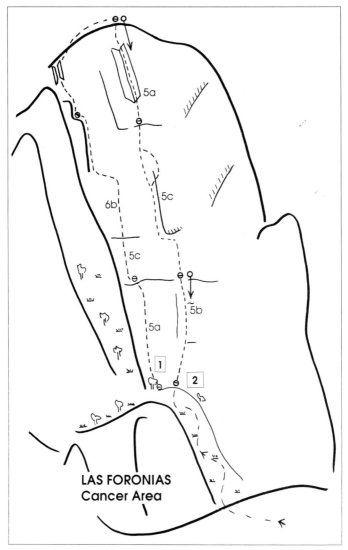

LAS FORONIAS
Cancer Area

La Mano Blanca, Las Foronias.
Climber: D.L. Walker
Photo: A. Harman

14.   La Mano Sangrando (The Bleeding Hand).   HVS. 5a.   45m.
1st Ascent: 13th April 1987 - D.L.Walker, I.R.Jones and D.Gale.

Devious but pleasant.

15.   La Mano Blanca (The White Hand).   E1.   5b. 100m.   **
1st Ascent: August 1985 - D.L.Walker and S.Smith.

Excellent protection.

16.   Esmeralda.   HVS.   4c. 50m.
1st Ascent: 18th April 1987 - C.Nunn and D.Gale.

A good line which will improve.

17.   Los Chicos Estan de Vuelta (The Boys are Back in Town).   E1.   5b.   ***
1st Ascent: 1st January 1987 - D.L.Walker and I.R.Jones.

Good positions in the middle of the slab.

18.   Stone Cold Sweat (Frio Frio Sudor).   E1.   5b.   45m. ***
1st Ascent: 22nd December 1986 - I.R.Jones and D.L.Walker.

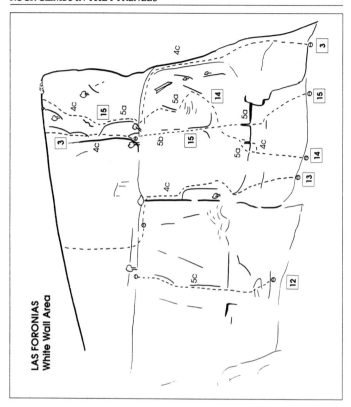

LAS FORONIAS
White Wall Area

A very bold lead on the first (boltless) ascent.

19.   La Mano Negra (The Black Hand).   E1.   5b.   45m.   *
1st Ascent: Easter 1986 - D.L.Walker and D.W.Walsh.

A much repeated route.

20.   Obsession Consumada.   E2.   5c.   45m.   *
1st Ascent: 1987

Thin and surprising.

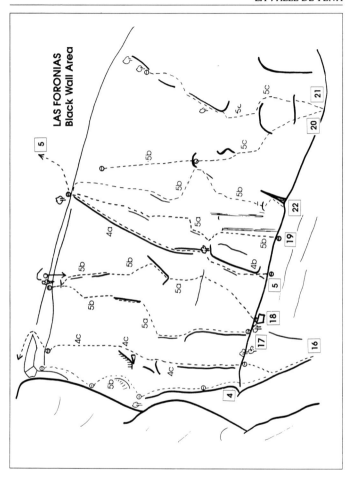

21. Digitalis. E2. 5c. 40m. *
1st Ascent: 1987 - D.Reade, Juan Varela-Nex and D.L.Walker.

Good but short.

THE SIERRA DE GUARA

This is a wilderness situated 20 km NE of Huesca and which itself is surrounded by the sierras Belarre, Aineto, Balces, Sevil and Gabardiella. Ravines and spectacular conglomerate and limestone towers and walls abound and the area is considered a beauty spot. There are a variety of outdoor pursuits to be experienced including 'gorge descending,' (see Appendix).

Within the Sierra de Guara lie two frequented climbing areas - Vadiello, mainly conglomerate and Rodellar (Mascun) limestone. However, there are walls, some of which are over 300m, as yet untouched, particularly in the Sierra de la Gabardiella.

VADIELLO
Here the conglomerate is very compact, finer than at Riglos, and the climbing is usually slabby or fingery, and of good quality. Most of the towers and spires were climbed in the 50's, but the majority of the routes were done in the mid 80's by T.Palacin, J.Olivan and B.Brun, using bolt runners because of the almost total lack of natural protection. The routes described have been chosen because of their length, quality or naturalness of line; however, several short routes are included as this is the style of present development. The new route potential here looks sufficient to last for decades and as at Riglos the atmosphere is made menacing by a sizeable army of vultures. There is a good picnic/camping spot at the foot of the Pared de Entrenamiento and a bar on the left of the approach road.

Turn north off the Huesca-Barbastro road at km 205, after passing an ancient hillside quarry and the conspicuous monastery of Monte Aragon (if approaching from Huesca). The signposts are for Bandalies then Santa Eulalia and eventually Vadiello. The road leads directly to the crags.

Pared de Entrenamiento
This wall is found by turning left immediately after the bridge and is made of very sound, dark grey conglomerate. A path leads from the small car park, meeting the stream and wall after about 100m at the foot of the buttress containing La Via Suerte Negra, easily identified by metal stakes leading up to the foot of the first pitch.

Descent from this buttress is by abseil back down the route and from the buttress to the right by a long traverse rightwards across easy ledges and slabs to well past the car park.

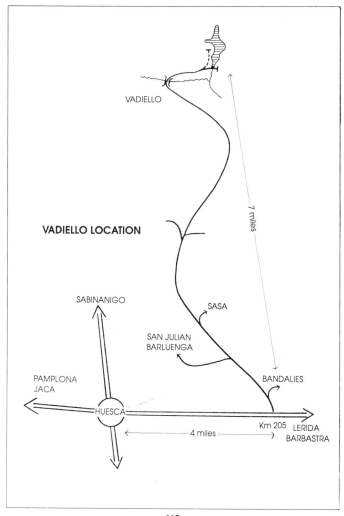

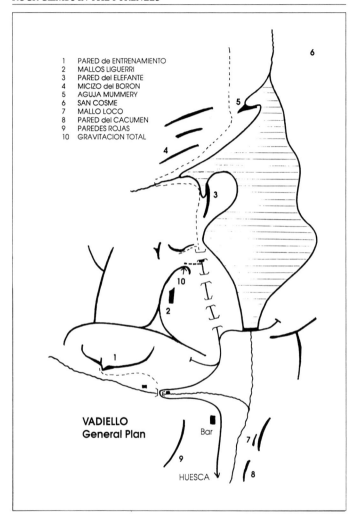

1   PARED de ENTRENAMIENTO
2   MALLOS LIGUERRI
3   PARED del ELEFANTE
4   MICIZO del BORON
5   AGUJA MUMMERY
6   SAN COSME
7   MALLO LOCO
8   PARED del CACUMEN
9   PAREDES ROJAS
10 GRAVITACION TOTAL

**VADIELLO
General Plan**

Bar

HUESCA

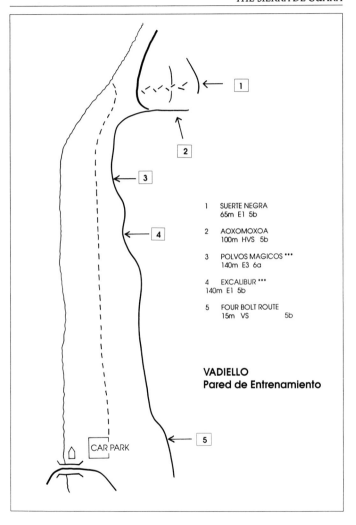

1   SUERTE NEGRA
    65m E1 5b

2   AOXOMOXOA
    100m HVS 5b

3   POLVOS MAGICOS •••
    140m E3 6a

4   EXCALIBUR •••
    140m E1 5b

5   FOUR BOLT ROUTE
    15m VS   5b

VADIELLO
Pared de Entrenamiento

CAR PARK

Vadiello from the approach road. Photo: I. Jones

Mallos de Liguerri
This central area is the highest, almost 300m, and consists of innumerable steep, bulging walls and towers of conglomerate whose quality is not as good as that of the Entrenamiento and Elefante. However, the **Mallo Puro, E1. 150m.** is a classic. It is best approached from the south via the small road which leads to the power engineer's building and then a couloir which leads to the col between the Puro and the face.

Descent is by abseil back down the route.
The road is blocked at the entrance to the last tunnel and to the left are a variety of short hard routes with their names at the foot, including **Gravitacion Total, E1. 5c,** immediately to the left of a small watercourse, **Sorros del Viento, 5c** and **Quebranta Huesos, 5a,** between Gravitacion and the road.

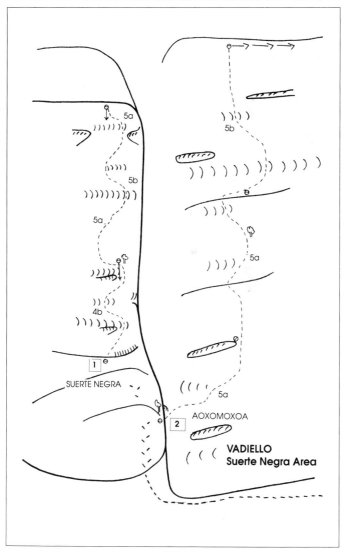

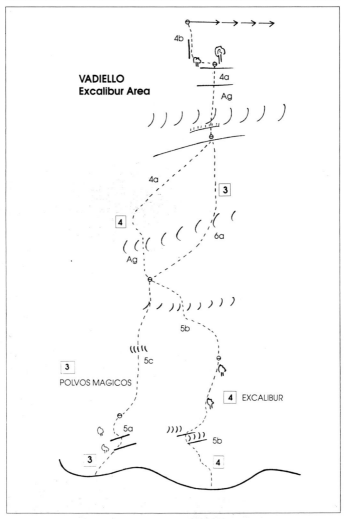

Vignemale North Face. Photo: Kev Reynolds
L to R. Pointe Chausenque, Piton Carré, Pique-Longue

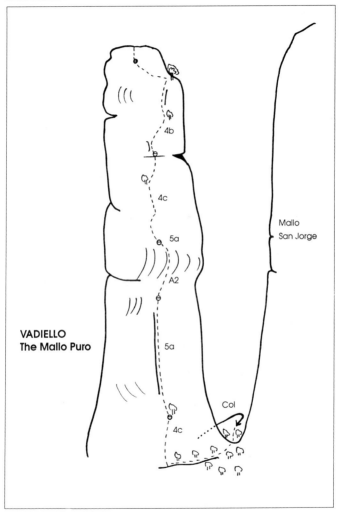

The traverse line on the Gruyêre slab, Santa Elena.
Climber: D.L. Walker Photo: A. Harman

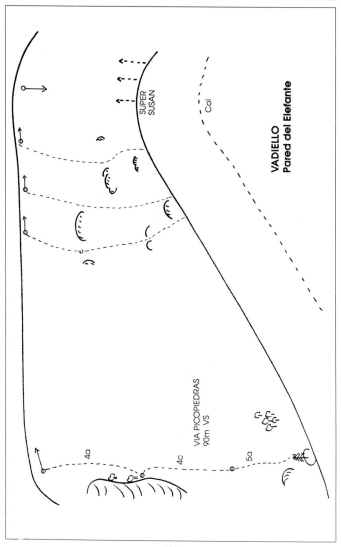

VADIELLO
Pared del Elefante

Col

SUPER SUSAN

VIA PICOPIEDRAS
90m VS

4a

4c

5a

Pared del Elefante

This aptly named wall faces west and gives short, high quality routes on excellent dark grey rock. There is a lot of development in this area.

Follow the path from the last tunnel up to a small col; the routes will be seen on the right and have their names written at their starts. Simply follow the bolts.

Super Susan.   E2.   6a.
Pera Limonera.   E1.   5c.
Platanito.   E1.   5c.
Asterix.   HVS.   5a.
Focus.   E1.   5c.
Via de las Truchas.   HVS.   5b.
La Via de las Picopiedras, VS. 5a, is situated 100m down from the col and provides an interesting logistic exercise in order to gain its start.

Descent is by abseil from a bolt station directly above Super Susan.

✳   ✳   ✳

LIMESTONE AREAS

The Cacumen, Loco, Rozas and Borón all have routes, but also a lengthy and painful approach by Vadiello standards. The Aguja Mummery has a spectacular North Face rising from the lake which is approached by a pleasant 30-minute walk.

1. **Original Route.**   HVS.   5a.   100m.
2. **Direct Route.**   HVS.   5a.   50m.
3. **Ziggy Stardust Finish.**   E1.   5b.   30m.

On the South Face is the **Via Cara Cartón, HVS. 5b. 30m.** This climbs a nice steep slab on the right arête.

Descent is by scramble back to the col.

123

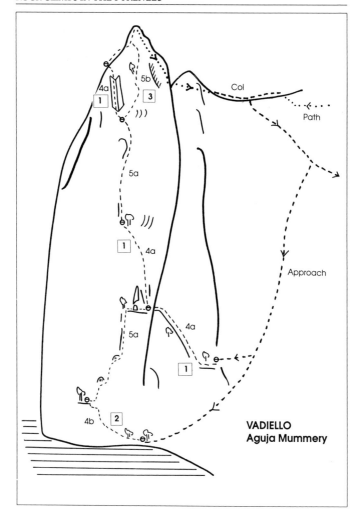

Col

Path

Approach

VADIELLO
Aguja Mummery

RODELLAR (MASCUN)

Leave the Huesca-Barbastro road at km 183, signpost for Rodellar and Colunga, pass through Abiega and Las Almunias de Rodellar before arriving at Rodellar itself. A variety of paths lead down to the river and the routes. A small campsite is situated by the road about 5 miles before the village.

Rodellar gives high standard, bolt protected, short routes on limestone in a setting reminiscent of the White Peak in Derbyshire. The area has long been a popular walking area and most of the more spectacular pinnacles were climbed in the 50's. Now the walls and cornices are being developed as a training area. The route names are frequently written at their bases and the café Florentino contains a new route book. However, due to the large number of routes, over a 100, and the usual haphazard nature of new route development, care must be taken when matching

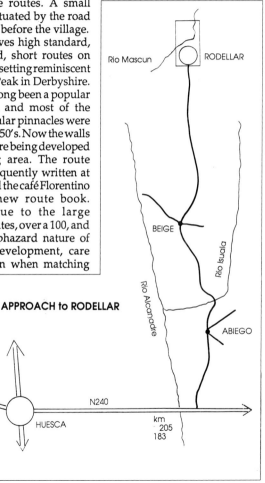

125

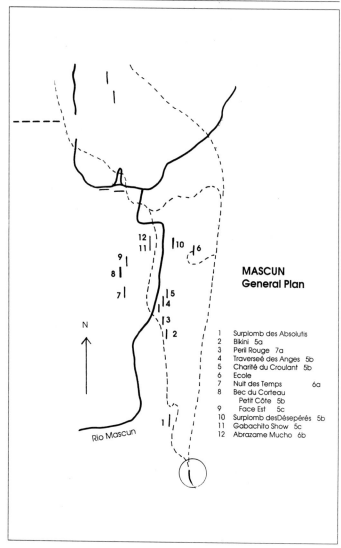

**MASCUN
General Plan**

N

Rio Mascun

1	Surplomb des Absolutis
2	Bikini 5a
3	Peril Rouge 7a
4	Traverseé des Anges 5b
5	Charité du Croulant 5b
6	Ecole
7	Nuit des Temps 6a
8	Bec du Corteau
	Petit Côte 5b
9	Face Est 5c
10	Surplomb desDésepérés 5b
11	Gabachito Show 5c
12	Abrazame Mucho 6b

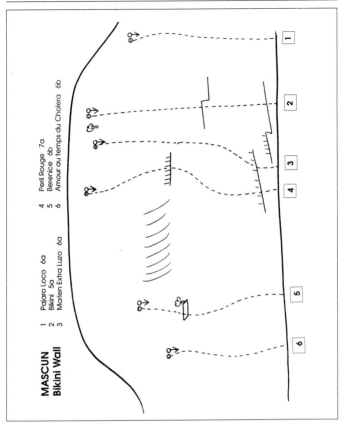

MASCUN
Bikini Wall

1 Pajaro Loco 6a
2 Bikini 5a
3 Marlen Extra Luzo 6a

4 Peril Rouge 7a
5 Berenice 6b
6 Amour au temps du Cholera 6b

the route book with the actual rock as many errors exist. The valley has a light hearted atmosphere and most climbers simply walk along the riverside and choose routes according to their appearance. Nevertheless, a map, diagram and short list have been included in order to aid the first time visitor.

APPENDIX

OTHER OUTDOOR PURSUITS INCLUDING GORGE DESCENDING

Skiing

Downhill skiing is catered for in Formigal and Panticosa. Cross-country skiing is popular in Balneario de Panticosa, on the Col de Portalet and in Ordesa. Ski mountaineering is the norm throughout the area. A typical day outing would be approach on skis, a medium snow/ice route using crampons and axes, followed by a downhill ski descent.

* * *

Hang-gliding and Para-gliding

The Panticosa ski-lift is operational through the summer and is used by hang-glider enthusiasts. The height gain required by para-glider pilots can be made by ski-lift, car along the high forest and pasture road or leg power. Many of the lower summits are grassy and rounded giving good take-off points.

* * *

Water Sports

Wind surfing is popular, particularly on lakes Bubal and Lanuza. Canoeists need a map and common sense with regard to water levels, bearing in mind the dam and reservoir situation in the area.

* * *

Gorge Descending

This is a mixutre of swimming, walking, scrambling and abseiling down river beds which can give a great deal of fun when resting from climbing and a change of activity is required.

The canyons and gorges, which are often invisible until one actually enters them, are huge - up to 200m deep and usually inescapable until the exit. The towering and frequently overhanging walls of limestone or conglomerate can be gazed at with the climber's eye for a new line almost indefinitely. Perhaps one day they will be developed? The occasional hermitage will be passed and numerous caves, some showing signs of ancient human habitation in the form of very early paintings.

The standards of difficulty can vary from simple outings of a few hours suitable for the whole family to major outings of several days needing much equipment and sub-aqua skills. The descents listed below, which are all in Sierra Guara, can be done in swimming costumes and training shoes, and serious techniques like the ability to recover an abseil rope while treading water in a moving pool above another waterfall, are not required.

However, care should **always** be taken as deaths occur in most years, even on the simplest of descents.

DESCENT OF THE VERO

This long but simple descent of a limestone gorge is very popular. Two cars are necessary, one being left at Alquezar, the other being used to transport the party to Lecina.

The road from Adahuesca to Arcusa via Colungo has a small side road to Lecina which crosses the Vero at a bridge alongside a campsite. Start here.

Purists walk down the river bed as opposed to the river bank. The point is academic as one soon has to cross and recross the flow. After 2 km make a committing 5/10m jump into a narrow, deep stream and swim 25m. The gorge continues for a further 6 km with other interesting delights including several gloomy sections through the impending cliffs. Several pots will be seen and are probably best avoided, the journey can be made as difficult or dangerous as takes one's fancy.

After about 4-8 hours an exit can be made at the bridge at Villacantal. However, it is preferable to continue down the river to a waterworks which is descended with both interest and danger and then a path immediately taken up to the right to arrive in Alquezar after a further 1/2 hour.

DESCENT OF THE MASCUN

This is a more difficult proposition than the Vero, requiring a more competent party, rope for a 30m abseil, cord for abseil points and wet suit vests in case the water is very cold, which it usually is.

Start and finish at Rodellar. The gorge descent starts at Letosa which is a 2¹/2-hour walk from Rodellar.

Descend to the Mascun and walk north for 1 km to the junction of three canyons. Take the middle canyon and after a kilometre, just before some spectacular spires, go up left, onto the plateau and follow the path to Otin, which is a further 3 km. Continue northwards for 3 km more, crossing the Gorge of the Raisin, to arrive in Letosa from the west.

The descent starts with an abseil of 30m down a waterfall, the 'Saltador de las Lañas.' Six hours of descent leads to the end of the difficulties and a further 2 hours to Rodellar.

NOTES

NOTES

CICERONE GUIDES

Cicerone publish a wide range of reliable guides to walking and climbing in
Britain - and other general interest books

LAKE DISTRICT - General Books
LAKELAND VILLAGES
WORDSWORTH'S DUDDON REVISITED
THE REGATTA MEN
REFLECTIONS ON THE LAKES
OUR CUMBRIA
PETTIE
THE HIGH FELLS OF LAKELAND
CONISTON COPPER A History
LAKELAND - A taste to remember (Recipes)
THE LOST RESORT?
CHRONICLES OF MILNTHORPE
LOST LANCASHIRE

LAKE DISTRICT - Guide Books
CASTLES IN CUMBRIA
WESTMORLAND HERITAGE WALK
IN SEARCH OF WESTMORLAND
CONISTON COPPER MINES
SCRAMBLES IN THE LAKE DISTRICT
MORE SCRAMBLES IN THE LAKE DISTRICT
WINTER CLIMBS IN THE LAKE DISTRICT
WALKS IN SILVERDALE/ARNSIDE
BIRDS OF MORECAMBE BAY
THE EDEN WAY

NORTHERN ENGLAND (outside the Lakes
THE YORKSHIRE DALES A walker's guide
WALKING IN THE SOUTH PENNINES
LAUGHS ALONG THE PENNINE WAY
WALKS IN THE YORKSHIRE DALES (2 VOL)
WALKS TO YORKSHIRE WATERFALLS
NORTH YORK MOORS Walks
THE CLEVELAND WAY & MISSING LINK
DOUGLAS VALLEY WAY
THE RIBBLE WAY
WALKING NORTHERN RAILWAYS EAST
WALKING NORTHERN RAILWAYS WEST
HERITAGE TRAILS IN NW ENGLAND
BIRDWATCHING ON MERSEYSIDE
THE LANCASTER CANAL
FIELD EXCURSIONS IN NW ENGLAND
ROCK CLIMBS LANCASHIRE & NW
THE ISLE OF MAN COASTAL PATH

DERBYSHIRE & EAST MIDLANDS
WHITE PEAK WALKS - 2 Vols
HIGH PEAK WALKS
WHITE PEAK WAY
KINDER LOG
THE VIKING WAY
THE DEVIL'S MILL (Novel)
WHISTLING CLOUGH (Novel)
WALES & WEST MIDLANDS
THE RIDGES OF SNOWDONIA
HILLWALKING IN SNOWDONIA
ASCENT OF SNOWDON
WELSH WINTER CLIMBS
SNOWDONIA WHITE WATER SEA & SURF
SCRAMBLES IN SNOWDONIA
ROCK CLIMBS IN WEST MIDLANDS
THE SHROPSHIRE HILLS A Walker's Guide
SOUTH & SOUTH WEST ENGLAND
WALKS IN KENT
THE WEALDWAY & VANGUARD WAY
SOUTH DOWNS WAY & DOWNS LINK
COTSWOLD WAY
WALKING ON DARTMOOR
SOUTH WEST WAY - 2 Vol
SCOTLAND
SCRAMBLES IN LOCHABER
SCRAMBLES IN SKYE
THE ISLAND OF RHUM
CAIRNGORMS WINTER CLIMBS
WINTER CLIMBS BEN NEVIS & GLENCOE
SCOTTISH RAILWAY WALKS
TORRIDON A Walker's Guide
SKI TOURING IN SCOTLAND

THE MOUNTAINS OF ENGLAND & WALES
VOL 1 WALES
VOL 2 ENGLAND

*Also a full range of guidebooks
to walking, scrambling, ice-climbing,
rock climbing, and other adventurous
pursuits in Europe*

*Other guides are constantly being added to the Cicerone List.
Available from bookshops, outdoor equipment shops or direct (send for price list)
from CICERONE, 2 POLICE SQUARE, MILNTHORPE, CUMBRIA, LA7 7PY*

CICERONE GUIDES

Cicerone publish a wide range of reliable guides to walking and climbing in Europe

FRANCE
TOUR OF MONT BLANC
CHAMONIX MONT BLANC - A Walking Guide
TOUR OF THE OISANS: GR54
WALKING THE FRENCH ALPS: GR5
THE CORSICAN HIGH LEVEL ROUTE: GR20
THE WAY OF ST JAMES: GR65
THE PYRENEAN TRAIL: GR10
TOUR OF THE QUEYRAS
ROCK CLIMBS IN THE VERDON

FRANCE / SPAIN
WALKS AND CLIMBS IN THE PYRENEES
ROCK CLIMBS IN THE PYRENEES

SPAIN
WALKS & CLIMBS IN THE PICOS DE EUROPA
WALKING IN MALLORCA
BIRDWATCHING IN MALLORCA
COSTA BLANCA CLIMBS

FRANCE / SWITZERLAND
THE JURA - Walking the High Route and
  Winter Ski Traverses

SWITZERLAND
WALKS IN THE ENGADINE
THE VALAIS - A Walking Guide
THE ALPINE PASS ROUTE

GERMANY / AUSTRIA
THE KALKALPEN TRAVERSE
KLETTERSTEIG - Scrambles
WALKING IN THE BLACK FOREST
MOUNTAIN WALKING IN AUSTRIA
WALKING IN THE SALZKAMMERGUT
KING LUDWIG WAY

ITALY
ALTA VIA - High Level Walkis in the Dolomites
VIA FERRATA - Scrambles in the Dolomites
ITALIAN ROCK - Selected Rock Climbs in
  Northern Italy
CLASSIC CLIMBS IN THE DOLOMITES

OTHER AREAS
THE MOUNTAINS OF GREECE - A Walker's
Guide
CRETE: Off the beaten track
Treks & Climbs in the mountains of RHUM &
PETRA, JORDAN
THE ATLAS MOUNTAINS

GENERAL OUTDOOR BOOKS
LANDSCAPE PHOTOGRAPHY
FIRST AID FOR HILLWALKERS
MOUNTAIN WEATHER
MOUNTAINEERING LITERATURE
SKI THE NORDIC WAY
THE ADVENTURE ALTERNATIVE

CANOEING
SNOWDONIA WILD WATER, SEA & SURF
WILDWATER CANOEING
A CANOEIST'S GUIDE TO NORTHERN
  ENGLAND (East)

CARTOON BOOKS
ON FOOT & FINGER
ON MORE FEET & FINGERS
LAUGHS ALONG THE PENNINE WAY

*Also a full range of guidebooks
to walking, scrambling, ice-climbing,
rock climbing, and other adventurous
pursuits in Britain and abroad*

CICERONE

*Other guides are constantly being added to the Cicerone List.
Available from bookshops, outdoor equipment shops or direct (send for price list)
from CICERONE, 2 POLICE SQUARE, MILNTHORPE, CUMBRIA, LA7 7PY*

Printed in Gt. Britain by
CARNMOR PRINT & DESIGN
95-97 LONDON RD. PRESTON